THE END OF IMPERIAL RUSSIA, 1855–1917

D0732465

European History in Perspective

General Editor: Jeremy Black

THE END OF IMPERIAL RUSSIA, 1855–1917

Peter Waldron

Reader in History
University of Sunderland

First published 1997 by
MACMILLAN PRESS LTD
Houndmills, Basingstoke, Hampshire RG21 6XS
and London
Companies and representatives
throughout the world

ISBN 0–333–60167–X hardcover
ISBN 0–333–60168–8 paperback

A catalogue record for this book is available
from the British Library.

This book is printed on paper suitable for recycling and
made from fully managed and sustained forest sources.

10	9	8	7	6	5	4	3	2	1
06	05	04	03	02	01	00	99	98	97

Printed in Hong Kong

 Published in the United States of America 1997 by
ST. MARTIN'S PRESS, INC.,
Scholarly and Reference Division
175 Fifth Avenue, New York, N.Y. 10010

ISBN 0–312–16536–6 (cloth)
ISBN 0–312–16537–4 (paperback)

CONTENTS

PREFACE

The disintegration of the Soviet Union, and the attendant downfall of the political system which had been created when Lenin and the Bolsheviks took power in October 1917, has engendered renewed interest in Tsarist Russia. Russians themselves have become able to examine the history of their own country with greater equanimity than was possible under the Soviet regime. The last decades of Tsarism have become the subject of considerable attention as contemporary Russia seeks to understand the circumstances which enabled the Bolsheviks to come to power.

The experience of imperial Russia also has a wider significance. Between 1855 and 1917 Russia changed dramatically. Modernization – political, economic and social – gripped the state as the old order tried to come to grips with a Europe-wide process of change stimulated by the twin cataclysms of political revolution in France in 1789 and of industrial revolution that left almost no part of the continent untouched. The Tsarist regime tried to maintain a difficult balancing act, torn between the desire to preserve its own authority intact and the need to cope with the stresses brought by rapid economic and social change. This was not a situation unique to nineteenth-century Russia: other contemporary regimes faced the same problems, while the twentieth century has witnessed numerous examples of the impact of economic modernization on political and social structures.

This book seeks to illuminate the chief issues that faced the people of the Russian Empire between 1855 and 1917. A huge, multinational state, playing a major role on the international stage, Russia was beset by all manner of challenges. By adopting a largely thematic approach, I have tried to draw attention to the continuities in the history of imperial Russia and to show the interplay of political, economic, social and international forces.

Since 1917, historians have debated many aspects of the history of imperial Russia and the origins of the Russian revolution at length and with great skill. Each generation of historians has sought to bring its own perspectives to bear on the problems of imperial Russia. History, however, is not made by historians but by the people of the past and it is their experience – whether peasant or Tsar, Moscow worker or Siberian colonist – that is of central concern to us. I have avoided direct reference to debates between historians: the bibliography provides pointers to enable the reader to get to grips with this dimension of the topic.

Writing a book of this type means drawing widely on the writings of others. I have tried to indicate my most significant sources in the notes and the bibliography, but must beg indulgence of colleagues whose contributions to my ideas I have failed to acknowledge. I am extremely grateful to Don MacRaild and Mike Rapport for reading the manuscript and offering many suggestions that have much improved it. Clare Crowley's comments on the text have been of very great value, as has been her support over the years.

Peter Waldron

NOTE ON NAMES AND DATES

Russian names are always difficult to deal with: I have used the familiar English version of the names of Tsars etc., but have left other names in their Russian form. Until February 1918, Russia operated the Julian calendar. In the nineteenth century, dates were 12 days behind the West and after 1900, 13 days behind. I have used the Russian calendar throughout and have added the Western equivalent where necessary in dealing with international affairs.

1

THE POLITICS OF AUTOCRACY

Russian political life before 1917 was overwhelmingly the preserve of social elites. The formal structures of government and bureaucracy were dominated by educated noblemen and it was their attitudes which continued to permeate the Russian political system.[1] The middle classes which were making their mark on the politics of Western Europe were much slower to emerge in Russia. In addition, the groups and individuals who manifested opposition to the autocracy came in large part from the same social background as those who made up the regime which they sought to reform or destroy.[2] The ordinary people of the Russian Empire played almost no part in institutional politics, and it was revolt – whether threatened or real – which most forcefully reminded the patriarchal Tsarist autocracy of their existence.

The structures of Russian government inherited by Tsar Alexander II on coming to the throne in 1855 were complex and reflected the ethos and principles on which the Russian autocracy was based. The Tsar stood at the head of the Russian state, ordained to his position by God, and with the unrestricted power to make whatever dispositions he wanted. This was not just a theoretical position, since no institutions had developed by the 1850s which could provide any sort of check to the Tsar's authority. Russian Tsars possessed the widest real authority of any European monarch in the mid-nineteenth century; the limitations placed on the powers of the English monarch in the 1640s and on the French after 1789 had found no parallel in Russia. The Russian state did not possess any form of representative assembly, nor any proper type of cabinet government. It was not law which guided the activities of the state, but the conscience and, indeed, whims of the monarchs themselves. Thus the three Tsars who ruled Russia between 1855 and 1917 – Alexander II, Alexander III and Nicholas II – were able to impose very different styles of government and to implement dramatic shifts in policy without having to gain the consent of any formal body. Alexander II made huge reforms to many of the key areas of Russian life, ranging from the abolition of serfdom to the introduction of a new system of courts, and was prepared to contemplate major constitutional reform 25 years after coming to the throne. His son, Alexander III, was of a quite different cast of mind and this, together with the terrorist assassination of his father which had brought him to the throne, ensured that his 13 years as Tsar saw deeply conservative policies being pursued.

The formal system of central government which existed in St Petersburg dated from the 1802 creation of a system of ministerial government. Ministries dealt with the traditional concerns of central government: finance, foreign affairs, justice and the like but, in contrast to Western European states, there was no institution which coordinated their work. Although a Committee of Ministers existed, its function was not that of a cabinet and it existed almost exclusively as an administrative body, rather than having any responsibility for policy-making. Individual ministers reported not to the Committee, but directly to the Tsar so that the monarch in effect acted as his own prime minister. The overall policy of the Russian government was, therefore, never formally discussed by the government as a whole and there was little consideration of the impact of one ministry's policies on the activities of other parts of the government. *Ad hoc* committees were established to deal with particular issues that needed wider consideration: in the late 1850s a whole series of bodies were set up to consider different aspects of the complex problems involved in the emancipation of the serfs, while proposals to reform rural local government drawn up in the 1880s came from a commission headed by Kakhanov, a senior bureaucrat. Whilst this method of organizing government business did ensure that key issues were debated in a wider forum than just the ministry in which they originated, Russian government continued to lack any mechanism by which policy could be consistently coordinated.

Such coordination of the work of the Russian government as did exist was achieved solely through the person of the monarch, but Russian Tsars hardly possessed a personal staff to support them in this task and to organize the complex work of governing the Empire.[3] The views and abilities of the monarch were critical, therefore, not just in setting the overall tone for the government but also in determining how efficiently the day-to-day work of governing the Empire was carried out. The personal qualities of the Tsar became especially significant at times when the Russian state was faced with crises or difficult decisions. Whilst Alexander II was prepared to grasp the nettle of serfdom in the late 1850s and to persevere to push through the long and complicated process of emancipation, Nicholas II found it difficult to act decisively and equivocated in making substantial reforms to cope with the waves of discontent which swept the Russian Empire during his reign.

In such a system it became easy, especially when the Tsar was weak or incompetent, for different ministries to pursue policies which ran at odds with each other. This was true on a large scale with the encouragement given to the process of industrialization in Russia by the Ministry of Finance, especially from the 1880s onwards. Successive finance ministers, and especially Sergei Witte during his term of office between 1892 and 1903, put in place policies designed to create an environment in which industry could flourish in Russia. Industry meant the establishment of large factories and the growth of towns and cities, creating concentrations of working people who often lived in difficult and unpleasant circumstances. The chief concern of the Ministry of Internal Affairs, however, was to maintain order in the Russian Empire and to ensure that the Tsarist regime was able to keep control of the population of the state. From the point of view of this section of the Russian government, policies to promote industrialization had important implications for the state's ability to maintain authority over its subjects. The growth in the urban population which was welcomed by the Ministry of Finance as evidence of Russia's growing economic strength caused concern to bureaucrats in the Ministry of Internal Affairs because it increased the likelihood of discontent and disturbances and posed questions about the ability of the government to deal effectively with outbreaks of social unrest. The Russian government never took an overall view of the consequences of its industrial policy. This deficiency was to have serious repercussions for the stability of the regime.

The ministers who staffed the government machine were responsible only to the Tsar. Each minister dealt individually with the monarch, meeting the Tsar regularly to deliver reports on the work of his department. These audiences were generally brief and often conducted without ministers submitting any form of written report in advance. The quantity and quality of the business which could be dealt with in such a situation was very variable, often reflecting the mood and interests of the Tsar. Ministers were wholly dependent on the monarch for their position: he appointed them and could dismiss them at will. V. N. Kokovtsov, Chairman of the Council of Ministers and a long-serving Minister of Finance, learnt of his removal from office in a letter from Nicholas II in 1914, the Tsar being unwilling to dispense with his minister 'during an unsettling interview' as he wrote.[4] It was extremely difficult for ministers to develop any sort of power base which would enable them to argue successfully with the monarch since he possessed the ultimate sanction of dismissal. This was seen in the case of Sergei Witte who, having been removed as Minister of Finance in 1903, returned to lead Russia's peace negotiations after the war with Japan and then played the key role in formulating the Russian government's response to the revolutionary uprisings of 1905. He so antagonized the Tsar during this process that Nicholas II took the first opportunity to accept Witte's resignation in April 1906, giving him only the most perfunctory thanks for the work that he had done to save the Tsarist regime from collapse.

The only institution which could play any formal and consistent part in advising Russian monarchs was the State Council. Established in 1810, the Council was intended as a consultative body to provide advice on legislation and the finances of the state. The State Council had no means of establishing itself as an independent body: until 1906 its members were all appointed by the Tsar and all came from the uppermost reaches of the bureaucracy. There was no compulsion on the Tsar to seek the opinion of the State Council on any matter whatsoever, and even if he did decide to take the views of the organization, he was at liberty to reject its conclusions or to side with the opinions expressed by a minority of its members. The State Council could, in certain limited areas, frustrate the monarch. Alexander III found it difficult to limit the judicial independence which had been granted in the 1860s, but the Council could only exert this type of influence in areas which directly concerned its membership of experienced bureaucrats.[5] Until 1906, when it was reformed, the State Council was often seen as providing a comfortable retirement for distinguished government servants.

The disconnected structures of Russian central government were mirrored when it came to local administration. The sheer size and variety of the Russian Empire meant that it was critical, if the state was to be effectively governed, for local government to be efficient and well-organized. This was not, however, the case. Local government existed on three major levels: the province, district and rural district (*volost*), but there was no conformity between the institutions which made up this system. European Russia was divided into 50 provinces each with a governor as the main agent of central government. There was no clear definition of the governor's exact status since he was the 'Tsar's viceroy' in his province as well as being the chief agent of the Ministry of Internal Affairs. As the former the governor had the right to inspect all government institutions in the province, irrespective of which ministry they came under, and to supervise the work of the elected local councils established in the 1860s and 1870s. His responsibilities as representative of a single ministry were also substantial: the governor chaired ten separate committees dealing with different aspects of provincial life ranging from the local statistical committee to the military service board. A senior civil servant wrote that 'The Russian governor could be the busiest man in the world, if the quantity of work he performed was measured by the number of official papers which passed through his hands',[6] for it was estimated that the governor's office dealt with upwards of 100 000 documents annually. In these circumstances, it is not surprising that governors varied very greatly in the diligence with which they approached their work and the effectiveness which they achieved.

Although each province was headed by an appointed official responsible to central government, there was no corresponding chain of command in the district. Although the average population of the districts into which each province was divided was approaching 200 000 by the end of the nineteenth century, the central figure there was the marshal of the nobility, a man elected by his fellow nobles and without any formal links to the government machine. This individual was the only unifying force in the district

6

administration, chairing 11 local committees and sitting as an ordinary member of 13 more. There was, however, no overall district administration board to oversee the work of government and neither central government nor the provincial governor had any direct authority over the unpaid and independent marshal of the nobility. The marshal's only direct subordinate was the police superintendent, an official who required no qualifications to be appointed, but whose responsibilities extended beyond the preservation of law and order to cover tax administration and collection.

The Russian government was well aware of the unsatisfactory way in which local government functioned; indeed improving the way in which the provinces were governed was one of its main preoccupations during the second half of the nineteenth century. In 1864 the Tsar took the important step of introducing elected local councils (*zemstva*) into most of the provinces and districts of European Russia. These councils were elected on a narrow franchise which ensured that the nobility would play the leading part in their activities, so that they comprised over 70 per cent of the members of the provincial councils and more than 40 per cent of the district *zemstva*. The councils were given rather general responsibilities: to deal with matters such as health, education, the maintenance of roads and bridges and local economic affairs. Their involvement in local affairs grew very substantially so that between 1876 and 1912 their expenditure grew sevenfold. This allowed councils to employ substantial numbers of teachers, doctors, agricultural experts and the like and this 'third element' of Russian local government (the other two were the elected council members and appointed government officials) came to play a prominent part in the life of provincial Russia. They acquired a reputation as radicals, partly because their frequent and close contact with the rural population resulted in their making demands for social reform and improvements in living conditions in the countryside. Local councils also represented an autonomous source of authority in imperial Russia, able to implement policies which did not necessarily coincide with those of the central government. Furthermore, once the principle of self-government had been conceded at the local level, the more liberal of the local councils argued that there was no reason why the same principle should not play a part in the national administration of the state. The activities of local councils provoked considerable disquiet amongst the central government, especially after the accession of Alexander III to the throne. In 1890 the councils' power to levy taxation was restricted and provincial governors were given the right to veto any appointments which the councils made. The relationship between the centre and these local elected bodies continued to be uneasy, especially during the revolutionary year of 1905.

Throughout the thousands of villages where most Russians lived, local government was constituted in a very different way. The sheer size of the Russian Empire meant that it was impracticable for the government in St Petersburg to try to exert close day-to-day control over the administration of the tens of millions of peasants in the countryside. Instead, the Russian peasantry enjoyed a considerable degree of control over their own affairs: each village had its own meeting of the heads of peasant households who elected one of their number to act as headman, responsible for collecting taxes in the village and for dealing with the most minor offences where the penalty was a very small fine or else a couple of days detention. After 1861 each village was part of one of 10 000 or so rural districts (*volost*) which included all the settlements within a diameter of about 25 miles. For every ten peasant households in the rural district, a representative was sent to the peasant meeting which then elected the district elder, who was responsible for maintaining law and order and for implementing the decisions of the district meeting. It was not easy to get peasants to take on these jobs as it was perceived that they entailed a heavy workload and meant the almost certain disapprobation of fellow peasants. Central government was not prepared, however, to see the administration of the great bulk of the peasantry exist outside its influence and local police officials were originally given the task of supervising the activities of village and rural district administration. The shortage of policemen, together with the evidence of poor administration by the peasants themselves, prompted Alexander III's government and especially the arch conservative Count D. A. Tolstoi, Minister of Internal Affairs from 1882 until his death in 1889, to introduce much closer supervision of peasant self-government. This was achieved in 1889 by appointing land captains who were able to overturn decisions made by peasant bodies, dismiss peasant officials and generally make the voice of central government felt in the villages and rural districts. The peasantry had no effective redress against the activities of the land captains, and this was made all the more significant by the judicial authority which the land captains held. Although this system of peasant self-government might be seen as essentially democratic, the ethos of arbitrary government which was the hallmark of the Russian autocracy permeated its institutions at the most local level. It ensured that, even before the advent of the land captain, the peasantry and their administrative institutions could be browbeaten by government officials and that the whims of the policeman, in particular, could have a huge impact on the peasants in his locality, much as the whims of the Tsar could affect the empire as a whole.

The same attitudes had been true of the Russian judicial system in the middle of the nineteenth century and Russian courts had been notorious for their corruption, delay and inefficiency. However, the change in the status of the peasantry brought about by the emancipation of the serfs in 1861 and the emergence of each previously enserfed peasant as a legal entity, free from the ownership of the landlords, meant that they had to be granted access to the law and this prompted a fundamental review of the whole imperial legal structure. In 1864 a system of civil and criminal courts based on Western models was introduced, with clear lines of appeal and staffed by a judiciary whose independence was assured through good salaries, thus obviating the need to take bribes, and by their irremovability from office. No longer could judges be dismissed for delivering verdicts which displeased the government. Furthermore, jury trials were introduced for the first time in criminal cases, thus introducing another element which was outside the control of the government into the administration of justice. During the 1860s and 1870s an independent and articulate legal profession came into existence, encouraged by the new freedoms which lawyers had gained under the reform and the courtroom became a focus for challenges to the authority and style of government of the autocracy. Lawyers came to be viewed by the regime as being in the same category as the *zemstvo* professionals – a source of autonomous opposition to the government – and the government made attempts to restrict their freedom. This proved more difficult than in the case of the local councils, however, since court proceedings could be openly reported in the press and speeches made by both defendants and their lawyers in the course of a trial could not be the basis for further prosecution.

These legal reforms had most effect on the populations of the large cities and especially on the judicial atmosphere in St Petersburg and Moscow, where the most significant and controversial trials took place. For the majority of the population, the peasantry, access to justice was rather different: those offences concerning solely peasants were dealt with by a village court, comprised of judges elected by and drawn from the peasantry themselves and operating under customary law. For minor disputes which concerned not only peasants, a system of Justices of the Peace (JPs) was established; these magistrates were elected by the district council and appeals against their decisions could be made to a higher authority. They proved to be of significant benefit in making justice more accessible to the population at large, since the JPs' courts worked quickly, cost nothing to those appearing in them and came to be perceived as delivering equitable judgements. Both in the setting up of a set of courts to try serious offences and in the establishment of a system for providing justice at the lower levels, the regime found that its aims of improving the judicial system and providing the peasantry with proper courts backfired. Whilst these aims were largely satisfied, the 1864 legal reform also laid the basis for a substantial challenge to the foundations of autocracy itself: the autocrat's power to act unconstrained by any other source of authority. Independent courts meant that such an independent source of authority did now exist, that the regime could no longer act in an arbitrary manner and, perhaps most importantly, that there was a clear recognition amongst the population that this was now the case. What the historian Wortman has called the 'development of a Russian legal consciousness' helped to weaken the Tsarist regime: instead of providing a buttress for the state, it gradually came to undermine the foundations of the autocracy.

In the same way as it moved to try to limit the authority of local councils, so Alexander III's government wanted to regain as much as possible of the power which had passed to the judicial system. It was difficult to interfere directly with the new legal structures; the guarantees of judicial independence and the watchful eye of the legal profession proved too strong for such direct action by the regime. Instead, the government moved to reduce the scope of the offences which were subject to the full rigours of the system. A major problem for the government had been that defendants accused of terrorist or political offences had used the new courts as a platform to make political speeches from the dock; speeches which were eagerly reported by sympathetic newspapers. Furthermore, the new juries had shown, in the government's eyes, a disturbing tendency to acquit people whom the regime would have preferred to see given long terms of imprisonment. The most celebrated of such cases was that of Vera Zasulich, accused in 1878 of attempting to murder the St Petersburg police chief. Zasulich admitted the offence but was sensationally acquitted by a jury which accepted her plea that the act was politically justified. This and other similar verdicts prompted the government to have as many as possible of these politically sensitive cases tried not in the civil courts, but through courts-martial. This avoided the publicity which the civil courts generated and it also reduced the risk that verdicts would be out of line with the government's own inclinations. The introduction of land captains was also part of this process; the land captain took over the judicial functions of the JP and the peasants who fell under his jurisdiction had no effective appeal against the decisions he made.

The institutions of administration and justice provided the framework for the maintenance of authority right across the empire. But the imperial government also relied heavily on coercion to control the population. The arbitrary ethos which permeated Russian government made it easier for the state to take whatever methods it felt necessary to maintain control without much fear of its actions being subject to effective scrutiny. At the most basic level, order in the villages was the responsibility of the local policeman. He maintained a watch over the functions of the system of peasant self-government and was able to exert considerable influence over the lives of individual peasants. The official description of police duties ran to over 400 pages and included many matters which brought the police into close and frequent contact with ordinary people. As well as having a responsibility for dealing with crime, the police also played a part in tax collection and in a multiplicity of affairs connected with agriculture and the local economy. Although the police had accumulated such wide-ranging responsibilities, they were very thin on the ground in the countryside. In 1857 the province of Iaroslavl, containing nearly one million inhabitants and covering some 14 000 square miles, had only 244 policemen and most of these were stationed in the towns, leaving the countryside largely without adequate policing.[7] The few policemen which the Russian Empire did possess were generally recognized as being of low quality; the job paid very poorly, no qualifications were required to become a policeman and no training was provided. The shortcomings of the Russian police had been recognized throughout the nineteenth century and the government made piecemeal reform in the 1870s to increase their numbers. There was an unwillingness, however, to take major steps to improve matters, largely because of the huge cost involved in establishing a large and efficient police force.[8] The government did devote more resources to the political police: the gendarmes, who concentrated on identifying and dealing with opposition to the regime itself. The gendarmes were separate from the ordinary police force and remained under the direct control of the Tsar's chancellery but, with the empire's police resources being thinly stretched, it was recognized that maintaining two separate forces was increasingly ineffective and in 1880 the two were united under the control of the Ministry of Internal Affairs.

The shortage of policemen and the lack of effective supervision of their activities gave the rural police especial latitude in their work. This was accentuated by the extra powers which they gained from 1881 with the introduction of states of emergency in substantial regions of the empire. From 1881 until 1917 about one-quarter of the population of the empire lived constantly under some form of state of emergency; a proportion which increased dramatically in the revolutionary years of 1905 and 1906. Under this regime, local authorities could issue regulations on any subject connected with the preservation of order and they could arrest, imprison and exile people whom they considered to be dangerous. These provisions were interpreted very widely indeed and could be used against anyone considered undesirable by the local policeman. A Justice of the Peace commented that they were

a terrifying weapon in the hands of the local administration, giving wide scope for settling personal scores, for revenge, for complete arbitrariness and lawlessness . . . the essential evil of this legislation is that the most valuable blessings of man, freedom and the inviolability of the individual, are entrusted to lowly police officials.[9]

At times of extreme crisis the imperial government had to call upon the army to restore or maintain order, especially during 1905 and 1906 when areas of the empire most affected by uprisings were placed under martial law. In some areas, notably the Baltic provinces, troops were allowed to rampage through the countryside, executing suspected rebels without even the merest formality of a trial. In other parts of the empire, courts-martial were used to try offenders, resulting in some 5000 death sentences in the years between 1905 and 1909.[10]

One of the Tsarist regime's central concerns was to maintain control over the flow of ideas and publications within and into the empire. During the reign of Nicholas I, the ethos of censorship had been firm and many writers had simply not attempted to publish works which they knew would offend the regime and bring penalties on themselves. Censorship in the first half of the nineteenth century was carried out before works were published and was the responsibility of the Ministry of Education. This duty sat unhappily with the ministry's main responsibilities and, as one Minister of Education commented, 'it is completely natural that as a result of its duty as a patron of literature [the Ministry] cannot act as a severe judge'.[11] In the early 1860s substantial changes were made to the system of censorship when the Ministry of Internal Affairs, already responsible for maintaining order through policing, gained control of the process. From 1865 censorship was carried out once a work had been printed. Thus, the onus for ensuring that publications were within bounds acceptable to the government was put on to authors and publishers. They could now be prosecuted in the courts if published works were deemed to be unsuitable and, in the case of periodicals, the government could simply impose administrative penalties without having to use the judicial system at all. Censorship continued, therefore, to be a key weapon in the state's attempts to keep control of its subjects and the flow of opinion.

The reforms of the 1860s to the way Russia was governed did represent a move towards modernizing the Russian state, but they also proved to be a starting point for further calls for change. The central theme of the demands for more wide-ranging political reform was for the greater inclusion of the empire's population in the decision-making process. Autocratic government in Russia had been fundamentally changed by the Great Reforms of the 1860s, since this had for the first time admitted the principle that elected representatives should play an important part in the government of the empire. Although elected self-government was only introduced for local councils, the solid autocratic front which the empire presented had been seriously breached. The creation of these autonomous centres of authority served to whet the appetite of Russian social elites for further influence. Ministers and senior bureaucrats were well aware of the crucial nature of the measures which had been taken during the 1860s and of the implications which they had for the government of the empire at national level. Projects to provide some form of popular participation in central government surfaced at regular intervals under Alexander II from inside the regime itself. Valuev, Minister of Internal Affairs between 1861 and 1868, suggested that a consultative congress of deputies could be established, including representatives from the local councils, and that members of the congress should sit in the State Council. The Tsar's brother, Grand Duke Konstantin Nikolaevich, came to believe that the only way to remove the causes of the discontent which manifested itself so strongly was to allow the most responsible sections of society to participate in the work of making legislation. He believed that a consultative assembly would help to bring Tsar and people closer together without restricting the powers of the autocracy since 'the government is not imposing any duty on itself, but when it feels it would be useful and necessary, it would be able to consult with people who know the real needs of the population'.[12]

This theme was continued in the 1870s by the head of the political police, P. A. Shuvalov. For the head of one of the most conservative institutions of the autocracy to contemplate popular participation in the work of government is a clear demonstration of the seriousness with which this issue was being treated during the 1860s and 1870s. Shuvalov believed that the autocratic state could enhance its support and at the same time strengthen Russian society by bringing the landed nobility into the political process and by taking measures which would increase their prosperity. All of these ideas were rejected by Alexander II who, even though he had made wide-ranging and fundamental reforms to the government of the empire, was not prepared to take the logical final step and allow his subjects to participate in central government. The Tsar did change his mind, however, at the end of the 1870s. In the spring of 1879 an assassination attempt on Alexander failed and the Tsar moved to take severe measures to suppress revolutionaries; measures which were intensified after a bomb went off in the Winter Palace in St Petersburg in February 1880. Count M. T. Loris-Melikov, who had seen distinguished service in the Russo-Turkish war of 1877–8, was appointed with wide powers to restore order, but also with the task of examining the causes of the revolutionary movement. Loris-Melikov characterized his approach as being a 'dictatorship of the heart' and he took seriously his commission to investigate why Russian society was so unstable that persistent attempts were made to assassinate the Emperor. As part of this task he prepared plans to involve popular representatives in government through consultative assemblies. This time, Alexander II was prepared to recognize the virtue of allowing his subjects some say in the way in which they were ruled and, in the middle of February 1881, he agreed that local councils should elect members to sit with appointed experts in commissions to provide advice on legislation. Before this could be put into effect, however, Alexander II met his death when terrorists threw a bomb at his carriage as he drove through the centre of St Petersburg on 1 March 1881. From the government's point of view, this marked the end of proposals to make fundamental reform for almost 25 years. The new Tsar, Alexander III, and his advisers put paid to Loris-Melikov's proposals by the end of April 1881 and government policy moved quickly towards intensifying repression and stressing Russia's conservative traditions. It was not, of course, only the government which was the source of proposals for change. Russian public opinion, although constrained by censorship and by an absence of opportunities for open political debate, was nevertheless lively and significant. The social elites of imperial Russia were articulate, well-educated and well-connected. Although the 30 years of Nicholas I's reign had been a period when high-profile journals had been suppressed by the government, there had still been a steady increase in the number of outlets for public opinion in terms of greater production of books and newspapers.[13] This trend continued in the second half of the nineteenth century; in the years between 1860 and 1914 the number of books published annually in the Russian Empire increased from 2085 to 32 338 and the number of Russian-language periodicals grew from 170 in 1860 to 606 in 1900.[14] Opinion could therefore circulate in an increasing number of forms, aided by the censorship reforms of 1865. The number of universities grew from six in 1860 to nine by 1914 with the number of students quadrupling to reach more than 16 000 by the beginning of the twentieth century, while the number of specialized institutes dealing with subjects such as mining, medicine and forestry doubled to 24 in the same period.[15] These institutions of higher education contributed to the growth of the intelligentsia and provided a vital means for the transmission of opinions amongst those people who were likely to become influential across a wide spectrum of Russian life. This was clearly understood by the government, especially since many ministers and senior bureaucrats had themselves received a university education and had first-hand experience of the atmosphere of Russian student life.

Although political parties were prohibited in Russia before 1905, Russian elites still found plenty of opportunities to engage in debate on political and social issues. The nobility of each province assembled each year to deal formally with matters affecting them as an estate and to elect their leaders. Tolstoi's description of such an annual meeting in *Anna Karenina* gives a clear picture of the intrigue of provincial politics as well as the range of topics – agriculture, local justice, the position of the nobility themselves – which interested his characters.[16] The local elected councils provided a further opportunity for the exchange of ideas and information, made all the more significant by the real power which these bodies possessed. Their position as the only elected institutions inside the Russian Empire gave many local councils the confidence to promote the cause of popular representation more widely. Liberal council members pressed for the councils to be given greater responsibilities and for the principle of self-government to be extended to the national government, thus 'crowning the edifice' of the local structures.

This process had begun during the 1860s but only acquired considerable momentum during the following decade. In 1879 liberal members of the Tver provincial council called for 'genuine self-government, the right of the inviolability of the person, an independent judiciary and freedom of the press' and the Poltava council stressed that 'only by joint efforts of the government and the entire zemstvo can we decisively overcome the propaganda undertaken by the enemies of government and society'.[17] Members of three provincial councils took part in a 'congress of zemstvo activists', held illegally in Moscow in April 1879 and organized by I. I. Petrunkevich, a member of the Chernigov provincial council who had strong family links with the province of

Tver. The congress, attended by less than 50 people, merely proposed a regular annual meeting to debate political questions. An assassination attempt on Alexander II while the congress was taking place resulted, however, in very sharp police reaction and the arrest of people suspected of 'political unreliability' including Petrunkevich. Loris-Melikov's brief period in office was accompanied by addresses from a number of councils calling for the opportunity to participate more fully in the work of government, and the assassination of Alexander II prompted some councils to stress that, in the words of the Tver provincial council, 'the invincible and mighty strength that the Russian Tsar and the Russian people always found in times of trouble was derived from a union between the representatives of the land and the Supreme Power'.[18] This 'zemstvo liberalism' declined in the decade after 1881: it was made very quickly clear that Alexander III and his ministers had no intention of taking any steps towards extending the role of popular representatives in Russia, while the assassination of the Emperor demonstrated the impossibility of compromise between this strand of moderate opinion and those who believed that violent revolution was the only way for Russia to advance.

Russian public opinion was also able to coalesce around a growing number of organizations which represented particular professional or social groups or which attracted individuals with special interests or expertise. In the 1850s the Imperial Russian Geographical Society had provided a meeting point for members of the St Petersburg elite interested in economic and ethnographic questions, and this had been an important breeding ground for the ideas that underlay the reforms of the 1860s. Various groups based on industrial, commercial and professional interests came into existence from the 1870s onwards, primarily to promote their own causes, but they also presented increasing opportunities for opinions to be exchanged and developed.

Moderate Russian political opinion during the second half of the nineteenth century was aimed largely at bringing about change through the existing structures of Russian politics. Noblemen and the as yet limited numbers of the Russian bourgeoisie wanted to gain some say in the way in which the Russian state was governed nationally. The failure of the 1825 Decembrist revolt to overthrow the Tsarist regime and the subsequent reactionary policies of Nicholas I had, however, alienated much of educated Russian society from the state. The intelligentsia overwhelmingly distrusted the autocracy, even when the regime was prepared to make reform, but intellectuals were never able to agree amongst themselves on the direction they wanted Russia to take.

For some Russian subjects the autocratic state itself was beyond reform. Revolutionaries in Russia in the second half of the nineteenth century made up a tiny proportion of the population. As few as 2000 people took part in the 1874 attempts to take the revolutionary message into the countryside by 'going to the people'. The People's Will (*Narodnaia Volia*), the organization which succeeded in assassinating Alexander II in 1881, had only 500 members along with several thousand more sympathisers.[19] Nonetheless, these groups did have an influence on Russia which was wholly disproportionate to their size, partly through their terrorist activities and partly through the largely illegal circulation of pamphlets and newspapers. The Emperor's assassination in 1881 had been but the latest in a series of attempts on his life and despite the regime's efforts to restrict the flow of information through censorship and customs controls on publications from abroad, clandestinely produced works reached deep into Russian educated society.[20]

Russian revolutionary thinking from 1855 until the mid-1880s was centred around two basic positions, not always compatible with each other. The most common belief espoused by those who promoted revolution in Russia was that the Russian peasantry should form the basis of the new society which would emerge after the destruction of the Tsarist regime. The early 1860s saw appeals such as 'Young Russia', calling for a federal-republican Russia, based on peasant communes[21] and the establishment of the Land and Liberty (*Zemlia i Volia*) group which demanded a genuine peasant reform in the wake of the 1861 emancipation of the serfs. Nikolai Chernyshevskii, author of the tendentious novel *What is to be Done?* and exiled to Siberia for 20 years after 1862, constructed a more complex theoretical model to explain the need for change in Russia and to justify the establishment of a society based on cooperatives in the new Russia. These rather isolated expressions of opinion were the forerunners, however, of the much broader Populist movement during the 1870s; it tried to move from the theoretical musings produced by a myriad of individuals and small groups to practical action to realize its aims. Populist thinkers believed that humankind was inherently good but that the Russian state had repressed its population to such an extent that this prevented the emergence of any type of just or fruitful society. The Russian peasantry, in the Populists' view, bore the brunt of oppression and it would be these same peasants who would form the basis of a new and equitable society. The peasant commune, already in existence in Russia, would lie at the heart of the post-revolutionary Russian state and the communal structure could be extended to transform Russia into a federal state arranged around these socialized and self-governing units. The Populists saw this as marking Russia out as being able to pursue a social and economic path which was different from the vigorous industrialization which had gripped Western Europe by the 1870s. The price which they saw the West paying for industrial growth was one which the Russian Populists believed to be too high. They felt that Russia's relatively low level of industrial development meant that the opportunity existed for Russia to avoid capitalism altogether and to move directly to an agrarian socialism.

The second element of revolutionary thinking was related to the means through which revolution could actually be achieved in Russia. A debate raged in the rarefied circles of the Russian revolutionary intelligentsia about the role of the revolutionary elite and how far the ordinary people of the Russian Empire had to make their own revolution. The concept of a revolutionary dictatorship which would seize political power and then make a social revolution was one which proved attractive in an environment where mass politics did not exist and where there was little prospect of generating mass support for revolution. The activities and writings of Sergei Nechaev and Peter Tkachev were important in developing this tradition: Nechaev set out elaborate plans for staging a revolution in Russia and emphasized the absolute commitment that must be demonstrated by those leading the process. For Tkachev the revolution had to be undertaken exclusively by this small group of committed revolutionaries and power would be seized through some form of terrorist conspiracy. This trend was accentuated by the failure of the movement to draw the Russian peasantry onto its side in the early 1870s. A small number of radicals – mainly students and former students – fanned out into villages in most of the provinces of European Russia in the summer of 1874, but found the peasants to whom they were addressing their message of revolution to be singularly unsympathetic to their cause. Instead of proving to be the naive and pliant material which the Populists had envisaged, the Russian peasantry turned out to highly resistant to condoning attacks on authority, demonstrating instead a solid faith in the Tsar.[22] Nearly 800 of these agitators were arrested during the summer, but what most disturbed the government was the effect which they had, not on the peasantry, but in inculcating radical views into the rural gentry and local officials.[23]

The inability of the Populists to gain popular support in the mid-1870s was repeated in 1881 when the murder of the Emperor by revolutionary terrorists failed to result in any form of popular uprising. Revolutionaries, therefore, faced a crisis in the 1880s and had to embark on a fundamental reassessment of their strategy. This was made the more urgent by the deeply conservative and repressive regime of Alexander III, which dealt swiftly and severely with those involved in the 1881 assassination. The police were increasingly active against revolutionaries during the 1880s, infiltrating their organizations and acting quickly to pre-empt conspiracies. In 1887 a plot to kill the new Tsar was uncovered, leading to the swift execution of five of its leaders, including Alexander Ulianov, a trauma which was to have a decisive impact on his then 17-year old brother Vladimir, soon to become better known under his revolutionary pseudonym of Lenin.[24] In addition, the fundamental Populist belief that Russia could avoid the process of industrialization and develop along a different path was being undermined by the growth of Russian industry and the way in which Russia was increasingly becoming integrated into the European industrial economy. The nature of opposition to the autocratic regime therefore underwent substantial changes during the 1880s and 1890s. Some of the chief proponents of agrarian socialism in Russia, such as Nikolai Mikhailovskii and V. P. Vorontsov, continued to believe that Russia need not experience capitalism, and these 'legal populists' suggested that a policy of 'small deeds' was the way forward instead of revolution. This meant using the institutions of the Russian state to bring about the greatest possible improvement in the life of the Russian people, in the belief that the state itself would gradually come to appreciate the benefits of a socialized economy. The contrast between this approach and the fiery words and deeds of the 1860s and 1870s was dramatic and suggested that change in Russia was not likely to occur quickly. For many Russian radicals, this was a deeply frustrating position and prompted them to look for other sources of inspiration.

The Marxist ideas which had been gaining currency amongst West European radicals found a ready audience in Russia. Marx's work had been known in Russia since the mid-1870s and in the wake of the failure of Russian radicals to enlist the support of the peasantry, Marx's emphasis on the role which would be played by the proletariat in initiating revolution was very welcome. Georgii Plekhanov, the 'father of Russian Marxism', had begun his radical career as a Populist but in the 1880s he moved sharply away from peasant-centred politics, writing that:

> The proletarian and the peasant are real political antipodes. The historical role of the proletariat is as revolutionary as that of the peasant is conservative . . . In a comparatively short time the proletariat has shaken the whole foundation of Western European society. And in Russia its development and political education is progressing incomparably more rapidly than in the West.[25]

The rapid industrialization that Russia was undergoing during the 1890s indicated that the country was set firmly on the capitalist path and, although Marx's theories suggested that capitalism had to reach its apogee before revolution could occur, Russian Marxists argued that Russia's special circumstances meant that change could come more quickly.

The existence of a tradition of revolt in Russia was seen as important in hastening revolution as was, paradoxically, Russia's backwardness. There was the prospect that Russia could utilize the advanced technology already developed in the West to shorten the time it took capitalism to develop fully. The initial work of Russian Marxists such as Plekhanov and Martov was based on the belief that Russian workers would come to take political action as a natural consequence of pursuing the economic grievances which had been intensified by the coming of an industrial economy. During the 1890s a number of organizations dominated by Social Democrat intellectuals came into existence: the St Petersburg League of Struggle for the Emancipation of the Working Class was founded in 1895 and was followed by similar bodies in Moscow and other cities. Some of these lasted only a few months and the weakness of workers' organizations, together with the impatience of Marxist intellectuals for political change, prompted some of them to adopt a different tack. It was vital to ensure political control of the nascent workers' movement, Lenin believed, and from 1900 onwards he argued that what was needed was a dedicated and disciplined party of committed revolutionaries who would lead the Russian working class. This elite would imbue the working people with a revolutionary consciousness and would mobilize them in the overthrow of autocracy. The tiny Russian Marxist parties of the first years of the twentieth century, their leaders mostly in exile abroad, were riven by splits and internecine argument largely carried on in an environment where there appeared to be no prospect whatsoever of their gaining power. Lenin's polemic *What is to be Done?* of 1902 and his proposals for a party programme proved to be a watershed in the history of the Russian revolutionary movement, bringing about a schism in the Russian Social Democratic party between his supporters – the Bolsheviks – who believed in an elitist party leading the working class, and those centred around Martov – the Mensheviks – who felt that the party should have a more equitable relationship with the workers in whose name it was acting. The Populist tradition remained significant in Russian political thinking. The Socialist Revolutionary party – the SRs – which was founded in 1901 embodied the Populist commitment to the peasantry by calling for all privately owned land to be distributed among peasant communes. The SRs believed that Russia could develop into an agrarian socialist state, since both the peasants and industrial workers would recognize its advantages and, once they were in a position to be able to express their will freely, they would undoubtably opt for socialism. The terrorist tradition of earlier revolutionaries was also reflected in the activities of the Maximalist wing of the SRs: they succeeded in murdering Dmitrii Sipiagin, the Minister of the Interior, in 1902 and his successor, Pleve, two years later, as well as committing many other atrocities. Despite having only a very loose party structure, the SRs could claim more than 350 000 adherents by 1907, while the Bolsheviks could muster only 35 000 members a decade later at the beginning of 1917. It was the SRs who emerged as the largest single party in the elections to the Constituent Assembly held at the end of 1917.

By the first years of the twentieth century the Russian political situation was much more complex than it had been half a century earlier. The regime itself displayed less sureness of touch; Alexander III died suddenly in 1894 and the new Emperor, Nicholas II, proved to be indecisive and unable to impose his authority with the vigour of his father. Although Nicholas possessed an overriding belief in the concept of autocracy and in the same conservative values as his father, his temperament made it difficult for him to put these values into practice effectively. In particular, Nicholas was easily influenced by his advisers and ministers and found it difficult to resist the views put to him by men of powerful personality. The situation was made more difficult for the Tsar by the increasing crises which struck the Russian Empire during his reign and which demanded the type of firm action which the Emperor was almost incapable of taking.

The Tsar's vacillations meant that the ministers whom he appointed during his reign represented a very wide variety of viewpoints. In July 1904 Viacheslav Pleve, the deeply conservative Minister of Internal Affairs, was assassinated by a bomb thrown by a member of the Socialist Revolutionary party. The Tsar took more than a month to make up his mind about a successor, apparently keen to replace Pleve with another arch-conservative, Boris Sturmer. But eventually he was persuaded to give the post to a man of diametrically opposed views, the liberal Peter Sviatopolk-Mirskii. The new minister made absolutely clear to Nicholas II the approach which he was likely to take, telling the Tsar that 'You know me but little and perhaps you consider me of like mind with the two previous ministers, but I am of completely opposite opinions.'[26] Less than five months later, Sviatopolk-Mirskii was replaced by a dull bureaucrat, Alexander Bulygin, who held the job for nine months before the highly conservative Peter Durnovo was appointed as Minister in October 1905. Even when dealing with the most significant ministerial appointment in the government, Nicholas II had extreme difficulty in deciding exactly what sort of policy he wanted to see pursued. Moreover, the very different ministerial appointments which the Emperor made during his reign only helped to contribute to the confusion and inconsistency in the regime's policies.

In the years between 1900 and the outbreak of the First World War, the Russian government swung sharply and frequently between reaction and reform. The assassination of Dmitrii Sipiagin, Minister of Internal Affairs, in April 1902 and the appointment of Pleve in his place brought about an increase in the role of the police in the Russian Empire as the regime intensified its attempts to eliminate opposition and to consolidate its position in the face of widespread discontent. Finland, part of the Russian Empire since 1808, was severely affected by measures designed to reduce its autonomy, while anti-Jewish pogroms, and especially the 1903 Kishinev massacre, produced only a muted response from the authorities.

During the 1890s the liberal elements of Russian society had begun to make a resurgence after the constraints placed upon their local government power-base. The famine and cholera epidemic which struck Russia in 1891 and 1892, leaving 400 000 people dead, and the government's inadequate response to these disasters spurred liberal opinion to action. A small number of senior local council activists began to meet secretly from 1898 in a group which became known as *Beseda* and which was the basis of a liberal constitutional movement. The development of this movement during the first few years of the twentieth century was aided by a growth in the number of professional organizations and conferences such as the National Exhibition of Domestic Craft and the Congress of Activists in the Field of Agronomic Aid. These provided meeting points for those who worked in the provinces, especially for local council employees – the Third Element – and proved to be a useful means of disseminating the views of those who led the 'Liberation Movement', often from exile abroad. Nascent Russian liberalism included a very wide range of opinions and its leaders, such as Pavel Miliukov and Ivan Petrunkevich, had to take pains to make their programme as inclusive as possible. The original 1902 programme published in the illegal newspaper *Osvobozhdenie* (Liberation), steered clear of controversy by avoiding calls for a constitution or a parliament by name, although it included an explicit demand for a representative legislative body. The question of how this was to be achieved was avoided; there was no consensus as to whether change could come from above, with the Tsar granting reform, or whether change would only come about as the result of pressure from below. Little by little the radical intelligentsia succeeded in moving the liberal movement to the left, so that when the Union of Liberation was formally established in 1903 it was intended as an underground organization, aimed at promoting revolution. This shift had come about as liberals had realized that the local councils where the movement had originated were unlikely to become motors of successful change in Russia and that more direct action was needed if reforms were to be achieved.

During 1904 liberal calls for change were made more openly, more loudly and more frequently than at any time previously. With Sviatopolk-Mirskii at the Ministry of the Interior, Russian liberals felt that they had some chance of seeing reform accomplished and pressed their case very strongly. A series of meetings, culminating in a *zemstvo* congress at the beginning of November, reiterated demands for a legislative assembly, and this was the signal for a series of nearly 50 meetings across Russia – the 'banquet' campaign – which passed similar resolutions.[27] These liberal views were given further circulation through an increasingly adventurous press and through the formation of a large number of professional organizations, catering for engineers, doctors and the like.

Vocal and articulate though they were, Russian liberals lacked sufficient strength to bring about change by themselves and reform only took place in 1905 as a result of pressure from a wider spectrum of society. Student demonstrations had become more frequent in the cities of the empire since 1899 with a much-publicized gathering taking place in St Petersburg in 1901 to commemorate the fortieth anniversary of the emancipation of the serfs. Furthermore, working people in Russia were beginning to express their discontent through strikes and demonstrations. Since the mid-1880s work stoppages had been of increasing concern to the government; in 1901 a strike at the Obukhov steelworks in St Petersburg culminated in clashes with troops and police, and the following year May Day marches were reported in many towns, including a major demonstration in the empire's chief oil producing centre of Baku.[28] Between 1902 and 1904 local authorities in many parts of the empire issued prohibitions on public meetings in an attempt to quell the growing discontent, accompanying this in Kharkov in January 1904 with a call to factory owners to be alert to the spread of seditious rumours among their workforce.[29] The Russian countryside also witnessed an upsurge in disturbances and particularly severe peasant uprisings took place in Poltava and Kharkov provinces in 1902, with more than 80 estates being attacked.[30]

The screw was tightened further on the Russian state by defeat in battle. In January 1904 Russia and Japan went to war over their competing ambitions in the Far East.[31] Russian military performance was uniformly disastrous: the initial Japanese attack dealt a severe blow to the Russian Far Eastern navy; by May the main Russian base at Port Arthur was besieged and it surrendered in December 1904. The battle of Mukden in March 1905 was a Japanese triumph. They delivered a shattering blow to the Russian navy in May 1905 at Tsushima by destroying the fleet sent from Europe to rescue Russian fortunes. The United States' proposal of peace negotiations was accepted by both sides in August 1905. The continuing defeats which Russia suffered caused a severe crisis of confidence in the Tsarist regime and demonstrated more clearly than anything else the weakness of the autocracy.

Soldiers returning from the Far East spread first-hand information about the defeat as they made the long journey back to their homes in European Russia.

It was, therefore, at a time when the Tsarist regime was already under severe stress that it was faced with an unprecedented upsurge in popular discontent. On 9 January 1905 a mass demonstration by striking St Petersburg workers, marching into the centre of the city to try to present a petition to the Tsar, was met by troops who fired indiscriminately into the crowds, killing 130 people and wounding over 400 more.[32] The events of 'Bloody Sunday' brought about mass disillusionment with the government, and rendered useless the very tentative steps which the regime had been taking towards meeting some of the demands articulated by the liberal opposition. In the middle of December 1904 the regime had promised some concessions, such as easing press censorship and allowing greater freedom of religion, but Nicholas II, acting on the advice of the wily Sergei Witte, the former Minister of Finance, had rejected granting members of local councils any form of participation in the work of central government. These concessions had met with a frosty response from liberal groups and the aftermath of the events of 9 January 1905 demonstrated that the autocracy would have to do far more before it could reassert its authority.

The strike movement spread very quickly through Russia in January 1905 as working people expressed their anger at the events in St Petersburg. More than 400 000 people took part in strikes during January alone,[33] and they were joined in their protests by students at most of the empire's higher education institutions. The industrial unrest continued throughout the year, subsiding at the height of the summer, but re-emerging with renewed vigour during the autumn so that during October 1905 nearly half a million people stopped work. These strikes were motivated by both economic and political concerns and their very varied motivation made it extremely difficult for the authorities to take any sort of action, other than pure coercion, that would solve the problem. Discontent was not confined to the factories, for an unparalleled wave of rural disturbances also hit the empire. During 1905 there were more than 3000 instances of peasant rebellion, affecting Russia acutely during the spring and early summer and reaching a peak of ferocity at the end of the year. These uprisings frequently involved the burning and destruction of landowners' estates, along with strikes by agricultural labourers and the seizure of pasture land and meadows.[34]

During 1905 the Russian state was assailed from all sides. The internal attacks on authority in both city and countryside combined with increasingly confident calls from the liberal opposition to threaten the very existence of the regime. This was not, however, a case of an articulate elite leading the 'dark masses'. In February 1905 the government invited the population of the empire to submit suggestions to improve the organization of the state. This effectively legalized the open discussion of political and economic issues and social groups right across the empire took advantage of the opportunity to submit petitions. Peasant petitions were mostly concerned with economic issues but they did also contain political demands. In general, these were more locally focused than the national liberal concern for a constitution, but expressed the peasants' desire to see their local conditions improved through measures such as the abolition of the land captains and better control over the police and government officials. Although some of the authorities did try to take action to prevent the peasantry from discussing economic and political issues,[35] once started this habit of discussion and petition was very hard indeed to halt.

The concessions which the regime gave during 1905 were wrested from it grudgingly. There was considerable debate inside the government about the best way of dealing with the revolution which threatened to engulf it; the policies of repression which the Russian state had relied upon were called into question by Witte who argued that instead of dealing with the symptoms of discontent, the government should address itself to the real causes of the strikes and rural uprisings.[36] Little by little the regime moved towards granting a constitution; in February the government announced that it would allow 'elected representatives of the people to take part in preliminary discussion of legislation', but when the details of the scheme were revealed in August its limitations were made clear. The State Duma, the national representative body, was only to be a consultative institution and elections were to be indirect with the franchise heavily skewed towards large landowners and the peasantry which would exclude workers and most urban inhabitants. The huge and renewed upsurge in discontent during the autumn forced the government to acknowledge that a consultative assembly was insufficient to satisfy its critics and Nicholas II accepted, albeit with severe reservations, that the Duma should be transformed into a legislative body. The October Manifesto which announced this change of heart also declared that the new Duma would be elected on a wider franchise than originally planned and that the Russian people should be granted basic civil rights, including freedom of speech, conscience, assembly and association.

The issuing of the October Manifesto did not put an end to popular unrest. On the contrary, violence intensified in the cities of the empire and Jews suffered particularly in more than 600 anti-Jewish pogroms. The climax of rural disturbances came in November and the unrest was noticeably more violent than earlier in the year. More dangerously for the regime, mutinies began to break out in the army and navy. During the last ten weeks of 1905 there were more than 200 instances of rebellion in the armed forces.[37] The ability of the government to exert control over the population of the empire was seriously in doubt in the late autumn of 1905. Regaining the loyalty of troops was vital if the autocracy was to survive; conditions of service were improved in the armed forces and the government demonstrated its determination to deal firmly with mutineers. Reform was not the only weapon which the regime used to reassert its authority.

The Russian state was not prepared to abandon its traditional policies of repression and the police and troops used considerable force to restore order. From 1905 until 1917 the relationship between reform and repression in the Russian state was exceptionally complex. After October 1905 the Tsar increasingly resented that he had been compelled to concede a legislative parliament which limited his autocratic power. No longer could the emperor act precisely as he wanted, for now legislation had to be approved by the Duma before it could become law. The government moved to limit the effect of this concession as soon as it seemed that order was being successfully restored to the empire in the spring of 1906. New Fundamental Laws for the empire were issued in April 1906. The State Council was reformed to become the second chamber in the legislative process, to be comprised of both members appointed by the Tsar and representatives elected by corporate bodies in the empire. This arrangement guaranteed that the State Council would be solidly conservative in outlook and able to block bills passed by the Duma, while the legislative process was capped by making the Tsar's approval the final condition for the enactment of a law.[38] The Fundamental Laws continued to describe the monarch as an 'autocrat', and he could issue emergency legislation when the Duma and State Council were in recess. Although such decrees had to be submitted to the legislature for approval within two months of it meeting again, the government deliberately used this power to allow field courts-martial to operate between August 1906 and April 1907 while the Duma was not sitting and let the legislation lapse rather than face its certain defeat by introducing it into the Duma.[39] More than 1000 death sentences were handed down by the field courts-martial during their eight months of existence. The budgetary powers of the legislature were severely circumscribed by the Fundamental Laws which exempted expenditure on the army, navy and imperial court from the Duma's jurisdiction.

Although the franchise for the first elections to the Duma was limited and had been devised with the intention that a conservative peasantry would cast its votes for candidates who would support the Tsarist regime, this judgement proved to be very wide of the mark. The First Duma which met in April 1906 was dominated by the Kadets – the Constitutional-Democratic party – the embodiment of the liberal movement and the Trudoviki, a largely peasant party more radical than the liberal Kadets. Government and Duma found themselves wholly at loggerheads and after less than three months the Duma was dissolved and an interval of more than six months interposed before the Second Duma was to meet. These new elections produced a body little different from its predecessor and the situation of deadlock was repeated. After little more than three months the Duma was again dissolved, but this time the government took more radical action to ensure that the composition of the Duma would be more in line with its own thinking. On 3 June 1907, the day after the Second Duma had been dissolved, the government illegally altered the franchise to reduce peasant participation and increase the representation given to landowners and urban property-owners.[40] This had a profound effect on the results of the elections for the Third Duma, which resulted in the representation of the left being dramatically reduced so that the Kadets and Trudoviki together made up only 15 per cent of the deputies. The largest single group in the new Duma was the Octobrists, a centre party which took its name from the October Manifesto of 1905 which had set up the legislative Duma, and which the government hoped would be a reliable ally. Parties on the right also gained substantial support, taking one-third of the seats.

While the Russian regime was concerned to ensure a pliant Duma and was also busy during 1906 and 1907 continuing its policies of repression, the government was also committed to making fundamental reforms. The constitutional changes of 1905 had also brought about for the first time the establishment of proper cabinet government, with the Council of Ministers transformed into a forum for the discussion of policy and its chairman taking the role of prime minister. Between 1906 and 1911 this post was occupied by Peter Stolypin who enunciated a policy of 'pacification and renewal' for Russia. He believed that the two parts of this policy had to run in parallel, for to relax the fight against terrorism would result in such havoc that reform could not be implemented, while to abandon reform would be to cease the attempt at removing the causes of the discontent which fed the revolutionary fervour. In 1906 and 1907 the government introduced a whole series of proposals into the Duma: a major agrarian reform; bills to extend civil rights; the reform of local government; changes to the education system; the reform of emergency powers; and a bill to reform local justice. Stolypin intended fundamentally to alter Russia through his reform programme. He believed that 'renewal must begin at the bottom'[41] and declared that his reforms were predicated on the creation of 'a wealthy, well-to-do peasantry, for where there is prosperity there is also, of course, enlightenment and real freedom'.[42] The transformation of Russia which Stolypin envisaged would bring into being a class of independent peasant landowners, freed from the shackles of the peasant commune. In addition, Stolypin argued that the Russian state itself had to be transformed so that the ethos of arbitrary government was swept away and replaced with a commitment by the state to being itself governed by law. These twin areas of reform were designed to remove the underlying causes of discontent and to establish the Tsarist state as a strong and modern institution.

Reformers did not, however, have the political field to themselves in Russia after 1905. Nicholas II himself believed that the constitutional changes of 1905 had been wrung out of him and were an affront to his God-given autocracy. The success of the regime's repressive policies during 1906 encouraged the Emperor and the conservative elite of Russia to believe that reform was no longer necessary and that the state could revert to its previous patterns of behaviour. There was also a considerable popular movement which supported the traditional position of the autocracy and which was able to mobilize considerable grass-roots support for the monarch. The new legislative processes proved to be cumbersome and, lacking a 'government party' in the Duma, the government found it very difficult to make progress with its legislative programme. It is indicative that the only one of Stolypin's reforms to come into force – the agrarian reform – was enacted outside the normal Duma procedure. The rest of the government's reforms fell by the wayside during 1908 and 1909 as Stolypin realized that, if he was to remain in power and retain the confidence of the Tsar, he had to move to the right. The post-1905 Russian system of government had moved some way towards moderating the autocracy, but in the last resort it was the monarch who was able to dismiss ministers and to whose opinions, therefore, ministers had to defer. In 1911 Stolypin was assassinated in mysterious circumstances and Russian government from then until the outbreak of war in 1914 reverted substantially to its pre-1905 character.

The existence of the Duma and of a cabinet-style Council of Ministers made very little difference to the underlying nature of the Russian state. The political elitism of Russian government was only very mildly moderated by the reforms of 1905 and the efforts made by opposition groups did not succeed in bringing about fundamental change before 1914. The autocratic state appeared to have a considerable reserve of strength after 1905 although, as quickly became clear, this was only superficial. The suppression of the revolution and the government's continuing refusal to distribute land to the peasantry had begun to drive a wedge between Tsar and people, as evidenced by the peasants' overwhelming refusal to vote for conservative parties in Duma elections.

As the constitutional reforms made in 1905 proved unable to bring about fundamental change to the Russian polity, so the articulate groups which had established a foothold in the political structures of the empire through the Duma became increasingly disillusioned. The appointment in January 1914 of the 75-year-old Ivan Goremykin as Chairman of the Council of Ministers, a post which he had briefly held a decade before, symbolized the mood of Russian government. In the Duma the parties of the centre, especially the Octobrists with their dedication to the principles of the 1905 constitutional changes, found it difficult to motivate their supporters in the face of the government's stonewalling against reform. Parties on the left, which succeeded in obtaining one-quarter of the seats in both Third and Fourth Dumas, were wholly ignored by the government. It was the right and those committed to Russian nationalism who found themselves in the ascendancy. By 1914 the politics of the Russian Empire had reached a state of deadlock. The autocracy believed that it had regained its pre-1905 position. Reform was off the agenda and the people of the Russian Empire felt that their political aspirations were frustrated.

2

FIELD AND FACTORY: THE RUSSIAN ECONOMY

Between 1860 and 1914 huge changes affected the economy of the Russian Empire. The population – already growing quickly before 1860 – more than doubled from 74 million to 175 million. The structure of the countryside, where most of this population made its living, underwent fundamental change in 1861 with the emancipation of the serfs and again in 1906 when peasants were allowed to establish their own farmsteads independent of the communal structures under which they had lived. Railways were built across Russia so that the 1600 km of track which had been laid by 1860 grew to a network of 70 000 km by 1914 and included the Trans-Siberian railway, linking Russia's Pacific coast to its European heartland. Heavy industry grew quickly; coal production increased more than a thousand-fold and more than ten times as much iron was being smelted in 1913 as had been in 1860.

The industrial growth which Russia experienced during this half-century paralleled the process of economic change which took place right across Europe during the nineteenth century. Russia, however, remained well behind other important states in almost every area of economic performance. Russian national per capita income in 1913 was only one-tenth that of the United States and one-fifth that of Britain. Although both Russia's agricultural and industrial output grew substantially, output per capita remained low. Three-quarters of the Russian labour force worked in agriculture, yet per capita grain output remained below that of Germany and the United States by 1913. Though Russia compared well with Austria-Hungary in terms of per capita grain output, in industrial terms Russia's per capita output was only half that of the Habsburg state's.[1] The backwardness of the Russian economy had its parallels in the social world: the level of infant mortality in Russia remained almost unchanged between 1860 and 1913, whereas every sizeable Western state witnessed a considerable increase in the number of children surviving their first year of life.

Throughout this period Russia was undeniably economically backward in comparison with every other Great Power. This had a considerable impact upon the way in which the Russian economy developed as Russia's elites sought to overcome this position. In practical terms, Russia's economic weakness bore a direct relation to her standing as a Great Power. Defeat in the Crimean War in the 1850s was a severe shock to the Russian state. The Congress of Berlin in 1878 showed that Russia was unable to diplomatically sustain its military success in the Balkan war of 1877–8. Defeat by Japan in the first years of the twentieth century was especially galling as Russia, portrayed as one of the great European powers, was humiliated by an Asian state. These successive reverses to Russia's position appeared to confirm its economic weakness and meant that both the Russian government and the state's social elites had a considerable interest in promoting economic growth and, it was hoped, thereby strengthening Russia's standing on the world stage. Overcoming backwardness could, therefore, have direct and practical results. There was also a less tangible motivation for Russia's elites to strive to improve the state's economic position. Backwardness was perceived as a national stigma which affected Russia and which meant that the Russian state was perceived as inferior by its neighbours. For the Russian nobles who regularly travelled abroad and who were exposed to Western European life and culture, Russia's economic backwardness appeared to lie at the root of the state's difficulties and it was believed that only by pursuing the goal of economic growth could Russia hope to stand on an equal footing in cultural terms with other states.

When Alexander II came to the throne in 1855 this problem of backwardness was most pronounced in the countryside. Imperial Russia was an agrarian-based economy; 90 per cent of the population lived in the countryside during the 1860s and this figure decreased only slowly, so that even by 1916 some 79 per cent were still rural dwellers. The rural population comprised many different groups of people: landed gentry; village clergy; and workers in the factories which were found dotted across the Russian countryside. But more than 90 per cent of people in the countryside were peasants and it was this enormous peasant population – around 100 million in 1897 – which dominated the Russian economy.[2] Consequently, the Russian government had to pay very close attention to the condition and dynamics of the peasant economy. The framework which the state provided, in terms of both legislation and overall economic policy, was vitally important in defining the nature of the environment within which the peasantry farmed and lived.

Economic considerations were important in the government's calculations, but the state also had other motivations in taking actions which would affect the economic condition of the peasant population. The prospect of peasant discontent and uprisings and the threat which this could pose to the government was never far from the minds of ministers and bureaucrats in considering agrarian matters. In the 1770s the regime of Catherine the Great had been shaken by the Pugachev revolt, a peasant rebellion focused along the Volga, which had demonstrated the real trouble that dissatisfied peasants could cause the Russian state. During the 1850s an increase in the number of rural disturbances was one of the reasons for the Russian government embarking on the process of emancipating the serfs. Alexander II, speaking in 1856, famously declared that 'it is better to begin abolishing serfdom from above than to wait for it to begin to abolish itself from below',[3] and the 70 or so isolated peasant uprisings annually between 1855 and 1861 served to confirm this view in the eyes of contemporaries. The impact which the peasantry could have on the actions of the government was reinforced in 1905. The 3000 rural uprisings recorded that year were instrumental in pushing the regime into making constitutional reform and also served to strengthen the hand of those inside the government who were pushing for the major agrarian reform which Peter Stolypin implemented in 1906. The relationship between state and peasantry was, therefore, crucial in defining the framework for Russian agriculture, but the impact which the state could have on the peasant economy was limited.

The state could not and did not control the everyday economic decisions taken by Russian peasants. It was the millions of individual peasants and individual peasant communities which made their own judgements about sowing and harvesting, about the rearing of livestock and the everyday business of farming which, when aggregated across the Russian Empire, determined the overall prosperity of Russian agriculture. Neither did the rural economy depend solely on agriculture. Especially in central Russia, most peasant households were involved in other forms of enterprise. Handicraft work such as knitting or wood-carving, work put out by factories like unwinding cotton or factory work and wage-labour, often seasonal, all contributed to the peasant economy. In some provinces, particularly those close to large cities and where industry was becoming established, the majority of peasant households derived an income from a source other than the land. Peasants made complex judgements about their own economic position and took steps to ensure that they maximized their own prosperity. The state's role in this process could only be to provide the legal and political environment in which these millions of individual decisions were taken.

By the 1850s the structure of Russian agriculture was extremely complex. Most Russian peasants lived under the complete control of others; private landowners owned more than 10 million male serfs by the late 1850s, but this was exceeded by the state's 13 million male peasants who, even though legally free, still existed under the control of their administrators. The millions of private serfs were the property of tens of thousands of different owners who were used as the state's agents to provide effective policing over the rural population. The system of serfdom had developed as the Russian state expanded territorially and found that it needed to exert control over the scattered population which lived on the lands that it conquered. It was beyond the resources of the Russian state to police huge expanses of sparsely populated land and it gradually transferred responsibility for controlling the rural population to the landowners. The institution of serfdom was never formally codified but legislation of 1649 had set out the framework which continued for the next two centuries. Enserfed peasants could not own property themselves; everything they did possess was regarded as being the property of their masters. Serfs could not leave their lords and, if they did succeed in absconding, they could be returned to their masters at any time. Serfowners could move their serfs around their estates at will and serfs possessed almost no rights as individuals. They had no access to the legal system of the empire and their master acted as policeman, judge and jury in dealing with matters of law concerning serfs. The government attempted to set out limits on the punishments which serfowners could impose on their serfs but it was very unlikely that contraventions of the law would ever be detected. Serfs could be sold by their master, with the proviso after 1833 that parents could not be separated by sale from their unmarried children. The system of serfdom allowed serfowners almost unlimited powers over their serfs and although the state did try to regulate the relationship between master and serf, the serf had no means of seeking effective redress against his master if he felt that he was being treated unjustly. Not all Russian serfowners dealt badly with their serfs, but there are sufficient examples of ill-treatment to suggest that life for very many serfs could be extremely unpleasant. The British observer, Donald Mackenzie Wallace, described one serfowner of his acquaintance as a 'legendary monster' who used corporal punishment mercilessly on his serfs and dealt with any who dared to express discontent by transporting them to Siberia or else forcing them to enter the army.[4] Other serfowners treated their serfs rather better, appreciating that their own prosperity could depend on the efforts which their serfs made in the fields.

By the 1850s the ways in which landowners utilized their serf population varied. Many set a global figure for each village which they owned, setting out the farmwork which had to be performed for the lord and the quantity of cash and produce which the village had to pay in addition. Others defined obligation in terms of each individual household. Whichever system was adopted, most Russian serfs worked three days a week on their master's land, although this could vary with the season. In some parts of Russia peasants did not have to perform farmwork during the winter, while it was common for additional work to be required at harvest-time. Complex arrangements had grown up to systematize labour services: in some parts of Russia the distance a serf had to travel to and from farmwork could be offset against the amount of work due. In most provinces if a serf had to travel more than 4 km to work then each kilometre travelled meant half an hour's less work. Some serfowners demanded extra work from their serfs for hay-making or harvesting and paid wages for it, while others set it off against the total labour obligation that a serf owed.

Only a minority of serfs were able to avoid labour service altogether and make up their obligations to their masters by paying quitrent. For the serf, quitrent – paying a cash sum in lieu of labour – was a more attractive option, as it freed the serf from the day-to-day control by the lord or his steward that labour services entailed. It also allowed the serf to decide which was the best way of earning the money which needed to be paid to the lord. Some serfs concentrated on farming the plots of land which they held for their own use from the lord, while others left their home village to work elsewhere. This latter course was especially common in the northern provinces of Russia where the poor soil and cold climate meant that agriculture was a precarious business and where the proximity of large towns provided opportunities for employment. In 1857 more than a million peasants were issued with internal passports which allowed them to move outside their villages, even though they had to continue to pay quitrent to their lords, giving an indication of the scale of wage-labour amongst the serf population. Some serfs discharged their obligations to their masters by acting as personal servants. Nearly 7 per cent of the serf population of the empire was in this category and they had perhaps the least enviable existence of any group of serfs. Wholly subject to the whims of their owners, they had no allotment of land to work themselves and therefore had not even this small independent means by which they could support themselves. The government had become concerned by the situation of the household serfs earlier in the nineteenth century, seeing them as a waste of productive capacity, but their numbers continued to increase as the wealthiest Russian nobility lived their luxurious life.

In contrast, the peasants who were controlled directly by the state lived rather differently. They were spread across the whole of European Russia and included almost every peasant in Siberia. These 'state peasants' had a dual status: on the one hand, they had to pay rent to the state for the use of the land which they farmed and were subject to limitations on travel and to the general restrictions which officious bureaucrats could impose. On the other hand, however, the state peasants enjoyed a rather better existence than did private serfs. A German traveller noted in 1843 that 'serfs or peasants belonging to landowners have more protection and security against the oppression, impositions and maltreatment of officials than the state peasants',[5] and the abuses which officials could wreak on the peasantry were recognized by central government. State peasants did not have to perform labour services and reforms during the 1840s set out their position as 'free rural dwellers' rather than serfs of the state. Their lands were surveyed by the government and adjustments made to the size of their allotments so that, in general, state peasants had larger landholdings to work than did private serfs. The state peasants also found it easier to move off the land and work in factories and this helped make for a higher level of prosperity for them.

Farming in Russia was based on communal structures. The peasant commune was, before 1861, the body which was responsible to the lord for ensuring that the individual peasant's obligations had been fulfilled. Across much of Russia land could be repartitioned between members of the commune as household sizes and agricultural conditions changed. This affected the land which the peasantry themselves farmed to support themselves and to enable them to pay quitrent to the lord. It also meant that the system of agriculture was inefficient, since at each repartition, each household had to be provided with land of equal quality. Most Russian villages in the middle of the nineteenth century still utilized strip farming, thus ensuring that each peasant household got a proper share of both good land and the less fertile sections. Even in those areas where peasant land was not subject to periodic redistribution, each peasant household still had to fit in with the village's pattern of crop rotation and was not allowed to enclose its strips of land unless the peasant commune agreed. The agricultural techniques which the Russian peasant practised were therefore primitive and contributed to the backwardness of the agrarian sector as a whole.

It was the underlying physical conditions of the Russian lands which made agriculture such a difficult business and which had brought about the structures of serfdom and the state peasantry. The huge geographical expanse of the empire, the extreme climate, the difficulties of communication and the problems involved in external trade meant that farming could never be easy. The nature of the Russian state that developed across the vast expanses of territory made close control of the rural population a necessity, but one which could not be easily accomplished by the mechanisms of the state itself. The government could only rely upon noble landowners to carry out this task and serfdom proved to be the institution which most suited the landowners themselves, while it appeared to guarantee the state the security which it craved. The Russian system of agriculture therefore developed as a result of the peculiar geopolitical environment of Russia itself. Making reforms to the system therefore involved issues which struck at the very heart of the Russian state.

The structural issues of Russian agriculture persistently exercised the minds of the Russian political and social elite during the 1850s. In particular, they saw serfdom not just as a symptom of Russia's backwardness but as one of its causes. Serfdom came to symbolize all that was wrong with Russia and its replacement occupied the government for five years after Alexander II's accession to the throne. The attention paid to the legal framework of agriculture did nothing to help with the underlying problem of Russia's farms – their low yields. The overall quantity of agricultural produce which was grown on Russian farms had increased substantially over the eighteenth and nineteenth centuries as a result of more and more land coming under cultivation. But the grain yields that were produced per hectare in Russia compared very poorly with the productivity of agriculture elsewhere in Europe. By the mid-nineteenth century Russian grain production per hectare was less than half that of British, Belgian or Dutch farms and Prussia, France, Austria and Italy all succeeded in producing yields at least 50 per cent greater than Russia.[6] This problem was addressed only obliquely by the Russian government in the work which it undertook in the 1850s as it moved towards emancipating the serfs.

The impetus for embarking on the reform of 1861 which freed the private serfs came from, and was maintained by, the Emperor himself. The tangible problems of defeat in the Crimea and increased peasant discontent were intensified by great pressure from Russian social elites. Alexander II's aunt, the Grand Duchess Elena Pavlovna, hosted social gatherings at which prominent reformers met and exchanged views. An important segment of the Russian bureaucracy and intelligentsia agreed with Iurii Samarin, a prominent political conservative, that 'the problem of serfdom stands as a threat to the future and an obstacle in the present to significant improvement in any way'.[7] Russians in the 1850s believed that serfdom had to be abolished before any other substantive reform could be introduced; serfdom had acquired an importance which stretched far beyond the economic sphere. Official action to deal with serfdom was also prompted by the growing level of discontent which peasants themselves were displaying. Although the scale of peasant disturbances was still small during the 1850s, the number was growing. Between 1840 and 1844 there was an average of fewer than 30 disturbances a year on private landlords' estates; a figure which more than doubled in the following 15 years. In the late 1850s when emancipation was under serious consideration, the peasantry were the focus of attention and instances of discontent were carefully recorded. Rumours about the prospect of emancipation also prompted some peasants to try and take matters into their own hands. Even though the absolute number of disturbances remained low and was very far from posing a real threat, the sharp increase worried the government and acted as a spur to take action.

The process of emancipation was also driven by very high expectations of the economic results that would be achieved by the freeing of the serfs. As well as being seen as a precondition for further change, emancipation was also viewed as a panacea for Russia's economic ills. It was argued that the existence of serfdom acted as a brake on the Russian economy and that by abolishing it, the agrarian sector would be able to improve its performance as the serfs would be freed from the exactions of their masters and would therefore have the incentive to produce more. Russia's industrial progress would also benefit from emancipation, it was believed, by the removal of restrictions on peasant mobility which freeing the serfs implied. By releasing tens of millions of peasants from the ties which bound them to the land, a mobile labour force would be created, able to move to work in urban factories and thus allow Russian industry to progress quickly.

The debates which took place about emancipation during the late 1850s concentrated on reconciling the different interests among the Russian social elites. While the Emperor and many of his ministers were convinced of the need to free the serfs, emancipation would have a huge impact upon the serfowning nobility who were faced with the prospect of losing their tied labour and, possibly, part of their land. At the end of 1856 Alexander II appointed a committee to consider the peasant question. It met in secret to try to prevent the spread of rumour about the government's intentions and its initial attitude was far from radical. Prince Pavel Gagarin, a major serfowner, suggested that legal emancipation should take place but that the freed serfs should not receive any land. This followed the pattern of the process which had taken place in the Baltic provinces 40 years previously, which had resulted in the serfowners retaining their land and power but which had done very little to improve the condition of the peasantry. At the same time, the nobility in the north-western provinces of Kovno, Grodno and Vilna were being persuaded by the local governor, General V. I. Nazimov, to request formal permission from the Tsar to begin discussing how they might approach the peasant question in their own region. Alexander II's response to them in November 1857 was to allow the nobility to establish committees to debate proposals for the 'systematic improvement of the serfs' way of life'. These committees came into being not just in the three north-western provinces, but right across European Russia in the first half of 1858. Their conclusions demonstrated that there was a multiplicity of views amongst the provincial nobility about the way in which emancipation could be carried out, although the thrust of the committees' reports was, unsurprisingly, towards minimizing the impact of the measure on the nobility themselves. The nobility in general wanted to receive as much financial compensation for the loss of their serfs as possible and, in some cases, were keen to see the quantity of land which they would lose reduced to a minimum.

This disunity made it easier for the 'enlightened bureaucrats' at the centre in St Petersburg to determine the form which emancipation should take. This was helped by the stand taken by General Iakov Rostovtsev, a member of the secret committee, now renamed the Main Committee on Peasant Affairs, who had the ear of the Emperor. In the summer of 1858 Rostovtsev wrote to Alexander II to express his conviction that the serfs must be freed with land and that the state had to assist in the financial process by which this land would be transferred from noble landowners to their serfs. This proved to be a watershed in the process of peasant reform and Alexander II instructed the Main Committee that these principles were to form the basis of legislation. The transformation of principle into practice proved to be exceptionally complex. The Editing Commission which was established to prepare detailed statutes held more than 400 meetings over 18 months and produced 19 separate pieces of law to bring emancipation into law.

The legislation that was enacted in February 1861 declared that 'the serfdom of peasants settled on estate owners' landed properties, and of household serfs, is abolished forever',[8] and with this freedom came the right for peasants to carry on their lives without having to seek their master's approval for their every action. The process by which the freed peasants were to acquire land was, however, more gradual. For a

transitional period of two years the peasantry had to continue
providing either labour service or quitrent to their lords as
before, but during this period charters were to be drawn
up setting out the extent of the land which the peasants
would gain and the precise nature of the obligations which
they had owed to their lords. These details would form the
basis for the calculation of the financial part of the
emancipation settlement; the peasantry could buy the land
which they were allotted and they had to make redemption
payments for it over a period of 49 years, based not on the
value of the land itself, but on the extent of the obligations
which they had owed their lords. This did not mean that
the nobility would have to wait nearly half a century before
they would receive compensation for the land which their
former serfs would gain. The government realized that this
would not be acceptable to serfowners and so the state was
to advance most of the cost of the peasants' allotments to
the nobility immediately, although in interest-bearing bonds,
rather than in cash. Pressures on the state's finances meant
that the government refused to subsidize the process and
the redemption process had to be self-financing.[9]

Complicated formulae were set out to calculate the precise
size of the allotments which the peasants would receive. But
the landowner was allowed to reduce the size of these plots
if, after the removal of the peasant allotments, he would be
left with less than about half of his estate. As an alternative
to the normal process of land allocation, the peasantry could
opt to take an allotment about one-quarter of the size of
the norm without incurring redemption debts. These pieces
of land became known as 'beggar's holdings', anticipating
what fate held in store for those peasants who made this
choice. While the emancipation did give individual peasants
their legal freedom and the opportunity to own land, the
government remained extremely cautious of releasing the
tens of millions of serfs from all the bonds which restrained
them. The existing structure of the peasant village commune
was retained and substantially strengthened by subordinating

the individual agricultural and financial autonomy of its peasant members to the communal will. The traditional method of strip farming remained intact, and with it communal control over the growing of crops. Moreover, the commune's tax-collecting powers were extended to include responsibility for redemption payments so that the redemption debt was calculated for an entire commune, rather than individually. The commune therefore needed to retain as many members as possible to ensure that the redemption debt which each peasant household had to pay was kept as low as possible. In addition, there was no real incentive for an individual peasant to maximize his own income solely in order to pay off the redemption debt early, since each household's contribution was subsumed in the overall re-payment made by a commune, although peasants who had paid off their debt could ask to leave the commune.

The 1861 statutes covered only serfs of private landowners. It took a further five years for the government to proceed with the full emancipation of the state peasants, although the 1866 measures which enacted this took a somewhat different form. Instead of allowing the state peasants to move towards the outright ownership of the land they farmed, they were only to make a yearly rental payment for the use of the land. It took a further 20 years before an 1886 decision allowed the state peasants to begin a 45-year redemption process similar to that of the private serfs.

Emancipation did not produce the expected results. The initial reaction of the peasantry was largely one of confusion. As one provincial landowner put it, peasants belonging to wicked landlords 'could not believe that all the Tsar's mercy just consisted of them having to remain under this oppression for another two years'.[10] It took a considerable amount of persuasion before the peasantry became grudgingly reconciled to the two-year period of transition, and the need for them to pay for the land which they farmed was wholly at odds with the fundamental belief amongst the peasantry that, as they worked the land, they themselves were its real owners. While the freeing of the serfs did remove the psychological stigma of backwardness and paved the way for the other reforms of the 1860s, it did not bring about fundamental changes in the Russian economy. The yields which Russian agriculture produced remained dismally low: by the beginning of the twentieth century Russia's grain yields had slipped even further behind and were less than one-quarter of the British level.[11]

The continued failure of Russian agriculture to match West European levels of production was analysed minutely by very many observers of the rural scene. A. N. Engelgardt, a convinced radical, wrote in the mid-1870s that 'everything carries on as it was before the emancipation ... the only differences are that the quantity of plough-land has been reduced ... that cultivation is carried on even less well ... and the meadows are not kept in good condition'.[12] The government too was concerned by the apparent lack of progress which the agrarian sector was making and Witte declared that 'the reason which retards the firm establishment of the economy of our peasants is concealed in the legal conditions of their way of life'.[13] The famine which struck parts of European Russia in 1891 and 1892 spurred the government to examine again the structures of rural life, culminating in 1902 in the establishment of a commission to consider the needs of agriculture. This drew on the work of more than 600 local committees and resulted in a fundamental reappraisal of the emancipation settlement. The principle which underlay this work was a belief that the peasant commune had outlived its usefulness and that it was now acting as a brake on economic development, particularly through the stranglehold which it exerted on patterns of landholding and the consequent effect on innovation by the peasantry. The level of peasant disturbances during 1905 made it clear that the policing functions of the commune were insufficient to prevent major discontent and the results of the elections to the First Duma showed that the peasantry had espoused radical views with a vengeance.

Agrarian reform after 1900 was intended to deal with the same underlying economic problem as emancipation had been meant to solve, but it also acquired a crucial political significance. Peter Stolypin, who headed the government which came into being after the upheavals of 1905, believed that peasant prosperity was the key to political stability. If the Russian peasant could be enriched within the existing regime, then this was likely to put an end to unrest and negate the efforts being made by opposition groups to bring about radical reform or outright revolution. Stolypin's reform, rooted in his experience as a provincial landowner and official, was intended to allow the peasantry to break away from the commune by establishing their own smallholdings. Instead of village land being farmed as strips, the peasants who left the commune would be able to consolidate their holdings of land into a single unit, with the final stage being the establishment of the peasant's home on the newly consolidated farm. The Stolypin land reform enacted in November 1906 could not be implemented quickly. Although it was relatively easy for peasants to gain individual ownership of their land and to become legally separate from their neighbours in the commune, the process of physically disentangling their land from the commune was lengthy and cumbersome. Surveys of commune land had to be carried out and, when it came to establishing separate farmsteads for each peasant household, difficult negotiations had to take place to ensure that each household gained land which was of equivalent quality to the strips which they would surrender. The potential for disputes in this process was so great that the Saratov provincial marshal of the nobility, A. N. Naumov, devised a scheme which classified land by soil quality to provide an equitable basis for its distribution, a solution which was then recommended by the St Petersburg government to other regions.[14]

The response of the peasantry to the Stolypin reform was mixed. By the end of 1915, about one-tenth of the 12.3 million peasant households in Russia had set up independent farms, but only one-quarter of these had taken the final step and actually left the village to move their dwellings out of the village and onto their farmland. The onset of war in 1914 was one reason why the process of reform ground to a halt, but the Russian peasants themselves did not demonstrate overwhelming enthusiasm for the radical changes to the organization of their farms which the Stolypin reform represented. Even where farmsteads were formed wholly separate from the village settlement, there are many examples of them being occupied only seasonally so that the peasants returned to live in the village during the winter.[15] The attraction of the village community remained very strong, with the mutual assistance available when work on the land was hard, and the communal life of the village close at hand. Both the emancipation and the Stolypin reform were essentially legal attempts to resolve an economic problem and it is perhaps unsurprising that neither measure succeeded in bringing about the fundamental change which their progenitors intended. While change had to come to the organization of agriculture, the reforms of both 1861 and 1906 did not directly address the central problems of the Russian agrarian economy: low levels of production at a time when the population, especially in the cities, was growing apace.

The rural population did benefit in some ways from the changes to the framework of agriculture. Although the commune needed to ensure that taxation and redemption payments could be met without undue difficulty, this did not mean that it restricted the mobility of the peasantry. The growing cities of the empire were full of peasants: in 1890 over two-thirds of the population of St Petersburg had been born outside the city, a proportion exceeded among the Moscow population. About half of Moscow printers in 1907 still kept farms going in their home villages, while 90 per cent of them continued to send money back to support their relatives left behind on the land.[16] The intensification of communal structures after 1861 did not restrict the ability of the peasantry to move away from their rural base to find ways of maximizing their incomes; indeed it was in the interests of the commune to allow its members to do so. The emancipation also opened up the market for land. The peasantry could for the first time buy, sell and rent land without having to seek the permission of their lords. This legal freedom for the peasant coincided with large quantities of land owned by the nobility coming onto the market. Between 1863 and 1914 the amount of land owned by nobles in European Russia fell by nearly 50 million hectares, reducing their pre-emancipation total holdings by almost half.[17] This process was matched by a consistent increase in the amount of land which the peasantry were able to buy. Between 1877 and 1905 the amount of land owned by peasants, apart from their allotments under the emancipation, grew from 6 million to 21.6 million hectares.[18] This process was aided by the establishment in 1883 of the Peasant Land Bank, a government institution which assisted the peasantry to buy more land. Even so, the new bank only helped in 20 per cent of peasant land purchases in its first years, so that the peasantry themselves found the resources in most cases.

Even though Russia's grain yields were low by comparison with other states, the empire did succeed in increasing its agricultural production during the second half of the nineteenth century. In the five years after 1861 Russia produced 26 million tons of grain annually, which increased to 60 million tons annually in the five years before the outbreak of war in 1914. Although the population of the empire was growing at an annual rate of 1.5 per cent between 1883 and 1914, grain production expanded by 2.1 per cent annually. Even taking into account the rising level of grain exports from Russia, the net per capita production of grain still showed an increase over this period.[19] This apparently rosy picture does, however, conceal great variations in food production, both geographically and from year to year. In 1891 and 1892 famine was severe in the Volga and central agricultural region, with the provinces of Samara, Kazan and

Simbirsk suffering the greatest decline in their grain production.[20] Added to this, the years between 1905 and 1908 was a period when harvests were poor across much of Russia and grain production fell.

Much of the contemporary writing about the life of the Russian peasant in the late nineteenth century stresses the poverty and increasing misery which observers believed to be the main features of the Russian countryside. Boris Chicherin, a leading member of the liberal elite, wrote that 'the well-being of the peasantry temporarily improved in the first years after Emancipation, but then declined', blaming the peasants themselves whom he saw as characterized by 'family divisions, ruinous drunkenness and an inability to keep hold of money'.[21] A. I. Shingarev, a doctor later to become a minister in the Provisional Government during 1917, entitled his 1907 study of rural Russia 'The Dying Village' and a series of statistical studies carried out by local councils indicated a reduction in the amount of livestock possessed by the peasantry.[22] The peasant diet was described as 'meagre and simple'[23] and rural housing was regularly portrayed as primitive and unpleasant. Much of this 'literature of social lament' was based on personal observation of very limited areas of the Empire and many of those who described the condition of the peasantry did so from a standpoint of opposition to the Tsarist regime. This essentially anecdotal evidence presented from a particular point of view coloured the picture of the Russian peasant which was accepted by contemporaries and made an important contribution to the widespread conviction that an agrarian crisis gripped the Russian Empire.

There were considerable pressures on the peasant economy. The distribution of land after emancipation produced severe inequalities. Overall, the 1861 settlement resulted in the peasantry having about 4 per cent less land to work, but this concealed important regional differences. In the less fertile provinces of the north, north-east and east there was a substantial increase in the quantity of land which the peasants were allotted compared with their holdings as serfs. For peasants living in provinces with the most fertile land – those running from Poltava in the south-west to Kazan on the Volga – the allocation of land was much less generous. In parts of this area the allotment granted to the freed serfs was only two-thirds the size of the land they had worked before 1861. As well as this regional difference in land allotments, the 1.5 million personal serfs across the empire received no land at all, while a substantial number of peasants chose to take the 'beggar holding' of one-quarter of their previous allotment, free of redemption dues.[24] In the 1840s the Russian government had judged that the minimum allotment needed for subsistence was 5.5 hectares, but by 1877 more than 60 per cent of peasants had less land than this.[25] At the same time, however, the freed peasantry were increasing their land holdings by both buying land and renting additional allotments. By the turn of the century, half of the land on large gentry estates was leased and by 1905 the peasantry rented a total of over 40 million hectares; twice as much land as they had bought since emancipation. Only a minority of peasant households had both the need and the resources to rent additional land; in the 1880s about one-third of peasants took this course.

The extent to which peasants were able to increase their holdings was intimately connected with the price of land and the level of rents. Land prices began to fall during the 1880s, but increased again during the following decade with an especially sharp upturn in the second half of the 1890s. Prices then continued to increase until the outbreak of war in 1914. Rents lagged behind movements in prices; a fall in rents from the late 1880s was not reversed until the beginning of the twentieth century.[26] The peasantry were not, however, wholly impoverished by the increased price which they had to pay if they wanted to extend the amount of land which they farmed, since prices for agricultural produce went hand-in-hand with the cost of land. The amount of grain products which the peasants were able to keep for their own consumption showed an increase at the end of the nineteenth century, suggesting that the financial pressures on peasant households were easing, since a need for cash would have pushed the peasant farmer to sell as much as possible of his crop. This is underlined by the doubling in the quantity of wheat which the peasantry consumed themselves between 1885 and 1901: rye was the traditional staple peasant cereal and wheat commanded a high price on the open market. Nonetheless, peasant prosperity was far from being universal. Even in terms of agricultural resources, the Russian peasant experience was uneven in the decades before the outbreak of war in 1914. Although arable farming flourished, and grain production grew significantly, this was partly at the expense of rearing livestock. While the total quantity of horses, cattle, pigs and sheep increased between 1880 and 1914, the number per capita of each animal either fell or showed only a tiny increase.[27]

On balance, the peasantry were as a whole able to prosper from their farming between 1861 and 1914. Many peasants, however, worked as agricultural labourers and relied on these wages to support themselves, rather than living on the proceeds of their own farming. The 1897 census recorded nearly two million full-time agricultural labourers, but the nature of Russian agriculture meant that much seasonal help was needed, especially at harvest-time. There were probably several million more part-time farm-workers. Real wages for these agricultural labourers grew in money terms,[28] but the rising prices of agricultural produce meant that the prosperity of hired farm-workers fluctuated significantly.

It was not just agricultural conditions which affected the well-being of the Russian peasant; the government too exerted a powerful influence through the financial exactions which it levied on the Russian population. After emancipation, the freed peasantry were faced with the new burden of making redemption payments for the land which they had acquired, while direct taxation was levied both by central government and by local councils. Additionally, a variety of products were subject to indirect taxes. The level of redemption payments was calculated, not according to the value of the land which the freed peasants received, but in relation to the quitrent which the landlords were to lose (in 1862 labour service was converted into quitrent). This was originally designed to placate the landlords, by providing them with generous compensation for the loss of their serfs, but it meant that the peasantry's redemption payments were high in relation to the productivity of the land which they farmed. In these circumstances, it is not surprising that many peasants found it difficult to make redemption payments and arrears accumulated rapidly. By 1875 the level of arrears had reached 22 per cent of the annual amount due, and this continued to grow for the remainder of the decade. Although the government made successive reductions in the level of redemption payments during the 1880s and 1890s, arrears grew even more quickly so that by the end of the century they exceeded the annual amount which the peasants owed. Further attempts to reduce redemption payments in the first years of the century had little impact on the problem, so that one of the key components of the government's response to the revolutionary outbursts of 1905 was a decision in November 1905 to cut redemption payments by half for 1906 and to abolish them altogether the following year. Direct taxation levied by the St Petersburg government on the peasantry was also reduced by the abolition of the poll-tax in 1886. Levels of local taxation continued to grow, however, so that even though peasants were no longer making redemption payments by 1911, the total level of taxation to which they were subject was only very slightly lower than it had been 20 years earlier.[29]

Indirect taxes had a substantial impact on the peasant economy. The government levied them particularly on items which it would be difficult for the peasants to avoid purchasing: oil for heating and lighting, sugar, matches and tobacco. The largest single source of indirect taxation was, however, vodka. In 1863 the system of tax farming as a means of collecting liquor taxes was abolished and the government imposed excise duties on vodka. Revenue from liquor rose after 1863 and the abolition of tax farming eliminated the bureaucratic corruption endemic in the system.[30] The success of the 1863 reform encouraged the government to go one step further and introduce a state monopoly on the wholesale and retail trade in vodka in 1894. This move offered a further opportunity for the government to increase its revenue and by 1910 this single source of taxation was producing more than one-quarter of the entire revenue of the Russian state. Indirect taxes in general were much more important to the government's coffers than direct taxation and the revenue from these levies more than quadrupled between 1875 and 1914. Although the main source of these indirect taxes was from purchases made in the growing urban settlements of the empire,[31] this does not mean that it was the urban population which bought all the goods on which taxes were levied. There was continual movement of people between town and countryside and peasants were responsible for a substantial amount of the purchases made in cities. Thus, although the peasantry appeared to find it increasingly difficult to meet the redemption payments which they owed, their level of consumption of goods increased. This paradox can be partly explained by understanding the enormous regional variations in the condition of agriculture across the Russian Empire. The redemption payments for land in the less fertile areas on the peripheries of European Russia and the industrial provinces represented a much heavier burden than they did in more productive regions of central and southern Russia. Peasants in the fertile black-earth provinces were able to increase their income by bringing other land, for example meadow and pasture, into arable use and were, in any case, farming the most productive land in the empire. In contrast, it was much more difficult for peasants elsewhere to increase their agricultural production and they had to seek other sources of income to maintain their standard of living. There were also many differences between peasants living in the same region: peasants with smaller allotments suffered much more than those who had received larger plots of land, so that the peasant economy was a patchwork. Some peasants prospered, while others became more and more impoverished. Overall the Russian agricultural economy avoided crisis in the half-century after emancipation, despite the huge increase in the empire's population, and yet failed to make the spectacular progress anticipated from changes to the framework of rural life.

Although the agricultural sector dominated the imperial Russian economy, the process of industrialization which revolutionized European economies and societies during the nineteenth century did not leave Russia untouched. The Populist hope that Russia could avoid the social dislocation experienced in states in the West was already unrealistic by the time it was voiced in the 1870s. The commercial links between Russia and the West which had developed since the sixteenth century meant that Russia was an important component of the European economic system and was deeply affected by the increasingly rapid process of industrialization from 1750 onwards. The Russian state's desire to establish and maintain itself as a significant military power gave a considerable impetus to the process of stimulating the domestic industrial economy. This was assisted by the influx of foreign entrepreneurs who identified Russia as providing good opportunities for business.

By the middle of the nineteenth century the Russian textile and sugar industries were particularly advanced. The cotton industry produced more than 90 per cent of domestic demand while the woollen industry helped to satisfy both the army's need for uniforms – there were more than a million men under arms by 1860 – and the demand of the growing population for warm fabrics. Russia also reduced its reliance on imported sugar as its own processing industry increased its levels of mechanization and efficiency. This expanding sugar industry, concentrated in the Ukraine, was helped by the capital which local landowners were able to put into it.

It was the consumer industries which were most successful in the years before 1860; the early advantages which the Russian iron industry had enjoyed faded as it failed to keep pace with the technological advances which were being made in the West and lost its export markets. There were, then, elements in the Russian economy which promoted industrialization well before the emancipation of the serfs. The components of this 'autonomous growth stream'[32] included the growth of domestic markets, stimulated by the huge programme of expansion initiated at the beginning of the eighteenth century by Peter the Great. This process, as well as bringing more people into the orbit of the Russian state, also resulted in the improvement of communications both inside the expanding empire itself and internationally. Once industry had established a foothold in Russia, the new skills which came with the introduction of machinery and the establishment of factories were developed and refined. This process was aided by the development of technical education: colleges specializing in engineering and mining had been established since the first quarter of the eighteenth century, although student numbers remained small.

Although industry was able to grow as a result of these processes, the level of growth remained low and additional stimulus was required before Russian industry could hope to match the rates of expansion which Western Europe was experiencing during the nineteenth century. The Russian state had played an important part in promoting economic growth since Peter the Great had consciously embarked on his project to modernize Russia. During the early part of the nineteenth century, the Russian government adopted a much less engaged attitude to industrial development, standing back from direct involvement in economic decisions. But the situation changed after 1860. The government's decision to emancipate the serfs marked a turning point in its willingness to again take a direct interest in economic matters, especially since it believed that emancipation would have significant consequences not just for the agrarian economy, but also in promoting industrial development. Late nineteenth-century Russian governments, however, instead of investing directly in industrial enterprises concentrated on adjusting the overall economic framework to create as favourable an environment as possible for the growth of industry. This was not an easy objective to achieve, given the complexity of the Russian economy and the difficulty of identifying the impact of the government's actions on the progress of the economy.

Successive Russian finance ministers used a variety of means to try to influence economic decision-making. Directly under their control was the level of customs duties which could be levied on goods imported into Russia. In the 1850s and 1860s tariffs were reduced on many items as part of a general attempt to liberalize economic policy. This had the effect of making it cheap to import both raw materials and manufactured goods and reduced the incentive for Russian domestic industry to develop. At the same time, tariff reductions meant a decline in government revenues and this too played a part in decisions to raise duties from the late 1870s onwards. In particular, the Russian government wanted to stimulate the development of the iron industry, since metal products were fundamental to the growth of almost every other industrial sector and were especially important for the construction of railways. Tariffs were first increased in 1878 and then progressively through the 1880s, leading to the 1891 introduction of a prohibitive tariff which raised the duty on raw materials to 30 per cent of their value. In the case of iron, this represented a more than five-fold increase in duty since 1868 and was of substantial benefit to the iron industry in southern Russia which was able to develop based on indigenous supplies of coal and iron.[33]

The growth of the Russian railway network played a key part both in encouraging commerce across the empire and as an important instrument of policy which the government could use to promote domestic industrial growth. In the decade after 1868 there had been a four-fold expansion in the railway network, taking the total length of track to more than 22 000 km. Although much of the Russian rail network was built and operated by private companies, the state was active particularly during the 1890s in making direct investments in the railway infrastructure. While Ivan Vyshnegradskii was Minister of Finance between 1886 and 1892 the government followed a policy of restraining public expenditure, a line which appeared justified when the regional famines of 1891 and 1892 placed severe pressures on the government's budget. Vyshnegradskii, however, suffered severe criticism over the high levels of import duties and taxes which he had introduced. This policy, together with his drive to increase grain exports to earn Russia valuable foreign currency, were perceived to have weakened the peasant economy and made it less able to cope with times of hardship. Vyshnegradskii left office in 1892. The transfer of Sergei Witte from the Ministry of Transport to the helm of the Finance ministry, however, marked a turning point in the state's attitude to railway finance. Witte had made his early career in railway management, moving into government in 1889, and was convinced of the need for the government to play a direct role in the further expansion of the railway network. The keystone of his work was the construction of the Trans-Siberian railway and this huge project accounted for a substantial proportion of the 25 000 km of new track which was laid in the 1890s. State expenditure on railway building also increased enormously under Witte: in the six years of Vyshnegradskii's period in office the government devoted an average of 50 million rubles annually to railways, but in the period between 1893 and 1900 this rose to more than 275 million rubles every year.[34] Expenditure on railways had a direct and rapid impact on the development of Russian heavy industry. The building of the Trans-Siberian railway alone involved 25 factories manufacturing 39 million rubles worth of rails and by 1903 more than 1500 locomotives and over 30 000 wagons had been produced for the project by Russian manufacturers. As well as direct government expenditure on railway infrastructure, the state also provided loans to help in the establishment of factories to produce the materials needed by the railway network.[35]

Although the Russian government did make some direct investments in industry, the state budget was far from being robust enough to support a comprehensive programme of industrial investment. More than 30 per cent of central government expenditure between 1900 and 1914 went on state-owned railways and the government's vodka monopoly, and only around 5 per cent of the budget was devoted to subsidizing private industry.[36] Other sources of capital were therefore of prime importance for Russian industry. The banking sector had been relatively undeveloped before 1860, but in the remaining years of the nineteenth century Russian banks progressed to take on much of the task of providing credit for nascent industry. In 1860 the State Bank was established and, as well as being a vital part of the state's financial structure, it also acted as a commercial bank which provided credit directly to enterprises. Joint stock banks began to be established from 1864 onwards so that 46 had been set up by 1900, with six large banks dominating the scene. This provided a mechanism by which capital could be made available, but until the 1890s many Russian businesses were able to rely on their own profits to reinvest in their enterprises, especially since the important textile, food and distribution companies were very lucrative. Domestic sources of capital were, however, insufficient to finance the great growth in heavy industry which was vital if Russia was to be able to compete effectively. The government recognized that Russia had to be able to attract foreign investment if it was to prosper.

Witte was particularly aware of the need to offer an attractive environment for foreign investors and appreciated both the need for political stability and for favourable economic conditions. The Franco-Russian alliance of 1894 helped to reassure French investors that they would be doing business with a friendly power, and Witte's efforts to bring about a stable Russian currency were also vital in ensuring that investment in Russia was a sensible economic decision for foreign investors. Russian gold reserves had been built up during the late 1880s and this had helped to anchor the value of the ruble; but Witte went further and in the years after 1894 he engineered currency measures which resulted in Russia adopting the gold standard for the ruble in 1897. This meant that exchange rates for the ruble were fixed against other gold-backed currencies and provided an important degree of security for foreign investors. By 1900 more than one-third of capital in Russian joint stock companies had been invested by foreigners and when industrial enterprises are considered separately, the figure was over 45 per cent.[37] Foreign investment in Russian industry brought more than simple financial benefits. The introduction of advanced technology from Western Europe was vital, especially in the metallurgical industries, and in some industrial sectors such as chemicals and electrical equipment foreign firms were able to dominate the Russian market by virtue of their technical skills.

The elements which made for the rapid growth of industry in Russia combined to provide spectacular growth during the 1890s. The average annual rate of growth reached 8 per cent during this decade, but then slowed during the first years of the twentieth century, as the international economy went into recession. Russian interest rates rose and share prices fell from 1899, with a simultaneous fall in output from basic industries such as iron, oil and coal. An important component of this decline was a reduction in government expenditure because of the need to contain the budget deficit and it was only after 1908 that industry began again to expand.

Even though Russian industry expanded considerably during the 1890s, the structure of the industrial economy did not undergo fundamental change. The textile sector remained critically important, accounting for nearly one-third of the entire Russian factory labour force and 28 per cent of industry's total output value by 1914. Even though heavy industry had developed during the 1890s, mining and metallurgical industries produced only half of the textile sector's output value. Industrial statistics collected before 1914 suggested that Russian factories were significantly larger in terms of the average number of workers they employed than similar enterprises in Western Europe. In 1907 the Russian factory employed nearly twice as many workers on average as did its counterpart in Germany. This, however, is misleading since Russian industry did not consist only of the large enterprises which came easily to the notice of officials and collectors of statistics. There was a long tradition of small-scale industrial production in Russia and this cottage industry is estimated to have involved at least seven million individuals by 1910.[38] Cottage industry was not a discrete sector of the economy, however, since it was very largely the preserve of the peasantry who produced a huge variety of manufactured goods at home. These goods were sometimes sold directly by the craftsman at fairs and markets, or often were produced as outwork for industrial enterprises and were marketed through the usual industrial channels. The onset of vigorous industrial growth affected some areas of cottage industry and meant that many craft workers earned less from their labour. It did not, however, mark the demise of small-scale industry in Russia: the huge expanses of the Russian Empire continued to mean that, even though communications had improved substantially, there was still an important place for local producers of goods to supply solely their local market.

The outbreak of war in 1914 had very mixed results for the Russian economy. Heavy government expenditure on armaments after 1908 had stimulated domestic industry, and the immediate impact of war was severe disruption. Foreign trade fell dramatically with the closure of borders with Germany and Austria-Hungary and the blockade of the Baltic. Manufacturing industry's output declined so that both consumer and heavy industries were affected. The railway network was overwhelmingly occupied with the process of mobilizing the Russian army so that transporting goods around the empire became difficult. Although the problems of trade and transport continued as the war progressed, manufacturing industry, and especially heavy industry, prospered. The demands of the military for weapons and ammunition resulted in the level of industrial production in 1916 being 20 per cent higher than in 1913. The Russian economy, in common with other combatant states, swung decisively away from producing consumer goods during the war years.

The Tsarist economy was honeycombed with fundamental and structural problems. Although Russia by 1913 was one of the great world economic powers in sheer size, in per capita terms her performance was miserable. The economy remained grossly skewed towards the agrarian sector, despite the great spurt of industrialization which had taken place at the end of the nineteenth century. Structurally, Russia possessed the features of an early industrializing economy and had yet to make the leap to effectively modernize her economic structures and performance. The aspirations of the Russian government and of the growing middle groups in Russian society were, however, to see Russia occupy a place equal to that of the other economic great powers. This presented difficulties, since the only method of achieving this was to promote industrialization, and industrial growth had implications which were not always welcome to Russian elites. The development of factories and the process of urbanization which accompanied this ran counter to the need to maintain control of the population which lay at the heart of the Russian state's concerns. Wholesale modernization of the economy was needed if the Russian Empire was to prosper, but the difficulties of undertaking this within an antiquated political structure created a tension which was never satisfactorily resolved. Industrial growth and agrarian reform created a social structure whose aspirations the Tsarist regime found it hard to meet.

3

THE TRANSFORMATION OF RUSSIAN SOCIETY

The pace of economic change in the Russian Empire during the last decades of the Tsarist regime was mirrored by huge upheavals to the way in which the Tsar's subjects lived. Social change left no family or individual in the empire untouched. By 1917 the face of the Russian countryside was deeply affected by the process of urbanization and its impact on the lives of the peasantry. The traditional role which the nobility had played in rural society also underwent dramatic shifts. The new towns and cities of the empire and the factory work on which they rested introduced a new social environment to which urban dwellers had to adapt. Russian society became increasingly complex in the second half of the nineteenth century, especially with the development of new groups in the middle, between the long-standing noble elites and the mass of peasants. These far-reaching changes to the social structure of the Russian Empire were to have important repercussions for the stability of the state.

The most fundamental social structures were, however, deep-rooted and slow to change and this too had its repercussions. The ethos which underlaid the Russian family and, indeed, the Russian state was patriarchal. The dominance of men was enshrined in law. Russian law gave the male almost unlimited authority within the family: the husband automatically stood at its head and his wife was compelled to obey and live with her husband. Women's rights were severely restricted: a married woman needed the agreement of her husband to take a job, enter higher education or to obtain a separate passport or identity document, although she did retain control of her own property. The head of the household also held complete economic authority over its other members as he had both legal and traditional responsibility for the management of the family's property. There were some circumstances where the male's authority could be challenged: if the head of a peasant household showed himself to be incompetent at managing the family's affairs – usually because of drunkenness – the peasant commune could intervene to transfer authority to another family member. When the head of a family died, inheritance law laid down that property was divided so that male descendants gained a far larger share than did women.[1] As property was inherited strictly through kinship lines, widows did not inherit the property of their husbands as of right and instead could only receive a small proportion of it, intended just to be sufficient to support them.

These legal buttresses of male power did not fully reflect the actual relation of men and women, especially in peasant society. The women in a peasant family had clearly defined tasks which were vital to the running of the household. As well as carrying out the domestic work of feeding and clothing the family and looking after children, women played a vital part in agricultural labour. At harvest-time especially, women's contribution was necessary if the household was to be able to cut and gather all its grain. Peasant women who were married to the head of a household did themselves possess substantial authority in the family. They usually held sway over domestic arrangements and continued to have responsibility for the children until they reached adulthood and it was then the matriarch who arranged marriages for them. These formal roles played by peasant women were reinforced by a less tangible function as 'caretakers of oral culture'.[2] Many of the songs, poems and stories that made up the strong Russian folklore tradition were transmitted by women and reflected the values and life of the Russian peasant.[3] This informal authority which peasant women held in the family and the household was important, even though legal authority remained firmly in the hands of men.

Russian peasants lived mainly in extended family groups. Typical of pre-industrial societies, this structure was essential in an agrarian economy where mechanization was almost unheard of and where the family's survival depended on manual labour to carry on the work of farming. Headed by the father, the peasant household would include his wife, his sons and their wives if they had married, and his unmarried daughters along with surviving grandparents. Division of the household usually took place on the death of the father, although in a substantial minority of cases, families did agree that a married son could leave and establish his own household while his father was still alive. There were usually sound economic reasons for a household to divide. If land holdings were of a good size division was easier, or if the household gained a significant part of its income from wage labour and was not wholly dependent on the land for its support, division could take place without endangering the livelihoods of any of the new households. Although the government tried in 1886 to limit household divisions by insisting that they needed the agreement of the village commune, the peasantry continued in the main to evade official interference in household matters. In 1897, when the first full census of the Russian Empire was taken, the average household in central Russia consisted of around five persons. Household size had been declining since 1861 as households had divided more frequently once serfdom had disappeared.

Marriage was almost universal for the bulk of the population in European Russia. More than 90 per cent of the peasant population aged between 30 and 40 in the central provinces were recorded as married in the 1897 census.[4] The Russian peasant also married early compared to Western counterparts. The average age of marriage for women was only 20, while most men married when they were a couple of years older. There was very strong pressure on the young Russian peasant to wed since marriage was seen as marking the transition to adulthood for young men, while families were keen to acquire the extra labour that a daughter-in-law represented.[5] Involvement in industrial work, whether on the farm or in a town, tended to delay the age of marriage as families were less keen to lose a daughter if they depended on her work to bring in wages. Early marriage helped to ensure that illegitimate births remained infrequent in peasant Russia, as did the widespread social disapproval of premarital pregnancy. Children's lives were often very short: nearly half of rural children died before they were five in the late nineteenth century[6] and although medical reformers tried to improve the standards of child-care, traditional patterns of child-rearing were very difficult to change.

Important forces were at work in imperial Russia which were acting to change these fundamental family relationships. The process of urbanization meant that peasants who moved into towns and cities were exposed to very different patterns of family life. Fewer townspeople married; if they did marry it was when they were significantly older, and they tended to have fewer children than peasants. For the many peasants who moved from country to city, the pressure to change their household structure was considerable. It was difficult for a migrant family to live in their own, separate accommodation as wages were low and the pace of domestic building in the growing cities lagged far behind the expansion of the urban population. Less than one-third of Moscow's population in 1882 lived in family units.[7] This did not mean that urban dwellers did not have families, for many people who moved to the cities to work continued to maintain a household in the countryside. This 'bifurcation'[8] of families meant that the urban working population was dominated by men who left their wives and children behind in their home villages. Women did move to the cities, but those who stayed permanently tended to be single. This pattern was changing, however, as migrant men became established in the towns and more married women moved into cities to join their husbands as living conditions began to improve. Consequently, the number of young children in cities increased: between 1871 and 1900 the proportion of children under five in Moscow increased by nearly 40 per cent.[9] Although the initial impact of urbanization was to seriously dislocate traditional family structures through the migration of the wage-earner, by the beginning of the twentieth century the peasant family was beginning to accommodate itself to the urban environment.

The process of economic change did, however, give some women the opportunity to break free from the constraints of rural life. Albeit, if they moved to work in a factory, the conditions of life could be as difficult as on the farm and a woman's subservient position in a rural household might simply be replaced by subordination to a male factory owner, some were able to use this as a stepping-stone to greater independence. Russia did not stand isolated from the nineteenth-century women's movements in countries to her west. Russian feminists became active during the 1860s. The first generation of the movement came from the educated elite of Russian society and began by seeking to improve the lot of needy women through philanthropic work. Women such as Anna Filosofova, Nadezhda Stasova and Mariia Trubnikova attempted to promote employment opportunities for women, but by the end of the 1860s the main impetus of the nascent women's movement was towards establishing opportunities in higher education for women. The government was far from sympathetic towards these aspirations, but in 1870 it did allow courses taught by university professors to be offered at a popular level. This did not satisfy Russian women who wanted a real opportunity to gain a university education and their continued pressure was rewarded by the opening in 1872 of Higher Courses for Women in Moscow. This was followed by similar courses at other Russian universities and those in St Petersburg proved especially popular, attracting over 900 students in 1881, drawn mainly from the gentry.[10] The advances which women had made during the 1870s were not, however, sustained. The much more conservative regime of Alexander III during the 1880s resulted in the closure of all women's university courses except those in St Petersburg and it was not until the turn of the century that women were again able to assert their position.

It was only after the events of 1905 and the first stirrings of a mass political culture that women were able to press the case for greater rights. The introduction of the Duma gave women encouragement to press for the vote, but these hopes were dashed by the changes to the electoral law when the Second Duma was dissolved in 1907. Women's organizations had, however, been springing up across Russia and it was no longer simply women from social elites who dom-inated them. Most of the 1035 delegates who attended the First All-Russian Congress of Women in St Petersburg in December 1908 came from middle groups in society: more than half the women earned their own living.[11] The Russian women's movement proved slower to take root than in Western Europe, but as elsewhere the First World War brought a substantial shift in women's positions in Russia. By 1917 women made up more than 40 per cent of the industrial labour force and the mobilization of more than 10 million peasant men meant that their labour was vital on Russian farms.[12]

The Tsar's subjects were not bound together solely by the ties of family and household. Wider community structures played a crucial role in cementing social groups. This was especially true of the peasantry for whom the village commune was central. More than 140 000 communes covered European

Russia and more than 80 per cent of peasant land was held communally. A typical commune included three to five small settlements and some 700 hectares of land. Communal tenure was less widespread in the Ukraine and western provinces and unknown in the Baltic provinces, but in the heartland of Russia itself communes owned some 95 per cent of peasant land after emancipation.[13] The role which the commune played in peasants' lives encompassed much more than the regulation of farming patterns. The commune collected taxes from its members and passed them on to local councils and to the state. It was responsible for organizing peasants into work parties to repair roads and bridges within the commune's boundaries. Police measures also fell within the commune's remit. The commune had to maintain public order and was also the main point of contact which the peasant had with the empire's legal system. It policed its own members, dealt with civil matters and with minor criminal cases which involved only peasants and was also responsible for meting out punishments such as fines or detention to those who had committed misdemeanours. Social matters also featured large in the commune's responsibilities. It had to provide aid for the sick, the old and orphaned children and to organize relief at times of famine. Such schools as existed in the Russian countryside were the concern of the commune and it also had to look after the local churches and their clergy. These formal roles were supplemented by the commune's less tangible, but equally important function as the representative of the collective interests of its peasant members to outside authority.

The commune's affairs were dealt with by an assembly of all the heads of households. This body usually came to decisions by consensus, although under the strong influence of the older peasants. These men acted as the means by which communal practice was transmitted from generation to generation and their experience was vital in ensuring that the commune took appropriate decisions. One of the village assembly's most important tasks was to elect the officials who

headed the commune. Every three years a village elder had
to be chosen, but many peasants sought to avoid election
to the post. Mackenzie Wallace noted at the end of the nineteenth century that

> the more laborious and well-to-do peasants, unless they
> wish to abuse their position directly or indirectly for their
> own advantage, try to escape election as office bearers and
> leave the administration in the hands of the less respectable
> members.[14]

Anton Chekhov in his 1897 story 'Peasants' depicts a village
elder who, although bad at keeping up with his own tax
payments, backed the authorities when it came to ensuring
that other peasants paid up and who

> liked the sense of power, which he could only display by
> severity. He was feared and heeded at village meetings.
> He was known to pounce on a drunk . . . tie his arms behind
> him and shove him in the lock-up.[15]

The elder's job was unattractive to many peasants as it
was the elder who was the main point of contact between
the commune and government authorities. Once a peasant
had become elder, he was often seen by the peasantry as
the representative of the authorities, and this placed him
in a difficult position so that although not a full-time
government official, he had significant responsibilities for
implementing government policies. Peasants were, however,
compelled to accept the post of elder, if it was offered to
them, and exceptions were only made in the case of those
who had already had the job, were ill or were aged more
than 60.[16]

The practical impact which the commune had on the lives
of its members was very considerable and was vital in
maintaining a sense of community amongst the peasantry.
The Russian peasant was accustomed to assisting fellow

members of the commune if they got into difficulties. One observer described the form that such help took in a village in the province of Riazan:

> The attitude of the commune to its members who suffer misfortune is mainly expressed in help in kind. Thus, after a fire or during the construction of a new cottage, near neighbours will use their carts to bring wood or bricks. Anyone whose house has burned down will receive the commune's permission to gather brushwood in the communal forest for fencing.[17]

The sense of community which such actions engendered was vital when it came to making the economic decisions which were critical for peasant life. When the communal assembly resolved on an agricultural policy, no member of the commune could stand apart and refuse to be bound by it. Repartitioning land between households was the most extreme measure which the commune could take, but this did not happen often. There were many variations in the frequency and extent of repartition. In the central agricultural region of Russia many communes retained the same pattern of land-holding from emancipation until 1917, and official statistics indicated that across the empire one-third of peasant households were members of communes where repartition did not take place after 1861. During the 1870s and 1880s there was a flurry of repartition activity, occasioned by the need to recognize the changes to household size and structure which had taken place in the years since land had been originally apportioned after 1861. The government was keen to ensure rural stability and moved in the late 1880s to restrict repartitioning, legislating in 1893 to set down a minimum interval of 12 years between repartitions.

Even though the redistribution of communal land was not a frequent occurrence, peasants were still bound to each other by the need to organize their farming jointly. The strip farming that predominated across Russia meant that peasant farmers had to coordinate their sowing and harvesting and had to agree which areas of land would be left fallow. There were regional variations in the way communes organized farming. In some provinces communes left their meadows undivided and then shared out the hay which was grown between the different households, while elsewhere meadows were divided between peasant families in the same way as other areas of land. Communal land tenure had mixed effects on the pace of change in farming techniques. Arguments for change had to be convincing if they were to persuade the commune's members of the need to innovate, but once an innovation had been agreed it could be implemented effectively. Contemporary investigators reported that peasants did not want to be seen to be lazy by their fellows and that they believed that communal projects would produce prosperity for the whole village.[18]

The Russian peasant commune was an extremely cohesive institution. It maintained a balance between collective activity and allowing its individual members a degree of flexibility in their lives, while providing social and economic security. Its structure and customs were not rigidly fixed by central government, but rather could be adapted to local and regional conditions. The democratic structures which governed the commune contrasted sharply with the autocratic ethos of the Russian state and, although the same patriarchal attitude lay at the heart of both state and commune, the commune proved far more resilient. It provided its members with the individual freedom to take economic decisions which could maximize their income and itself proved adaptable to changes in its demographic structure, so that the duties it demanded from each household would vary as the composition of the household changed. The commune's durability was evident after Stolypin's 1906 land reform when the proportion of peasant land held by communes only dropped from 73 per cent to 60 per cent,[19] despite the state actively encouraging peasants to set up their own individual farmsteads free from the hold of the commune. Peasants who left the countryside to work in towns sought to replicate communal structures both at work and at home. The peasant commune remained the basic element of rural Russian society right up until Soviet agriculture was collectivized at the end of the 1920s.

Religion also made a major contribution to the cohesion of rural society. The Russian Orthodox Church was the dominant religious organization in the empire, including 70 per cent of the population as its members and was staffed by some 100 000 clerics. The links between the local priest and his flock were very close, if somewhat strained, since the priest was dependent on his parish for providing him with sufficient income to support himself. Although the Orthodox Church was closely entangled with the state apparatus of imperial Russia, with its senior official – the Chief Procurator of the Holy Synod – appointed by the Tsar from the laity, the state had never assumed responsibility for the upkeep of the parish clergy. It was therefore vital for the priest to maintain the confidence and support of his flock if he was to continue to receive gifts and payments in money and produce, as well as help on the plot of church land from his parishioners. The involvement of the clergy in the work of farming – 'the principal source of income for priests', as one observer commented[20] – helped to reinforce the ties which bound the priest and his parish together. Not all priests, however, gained the respect of the Russian peasant and there are many reports of drunken and incompetent priests neglecting their religious duties and slipping into extreme poverty.

The parish clergy also had a role assigned to them by the state. They were a means by which central government could transmit its views to the population as a whole. A circular to all clerics in 1902 from the Holy Synod – the governing body of the Orthodox Church – instructed bishops to get their priests 'to explain to their congregations the falseness, according to the word of God, of the appeals of the evil-minded who urge them to disobey the authorities established by the Tsar and to attack the property of others'.[21] The state, however, was reluctant for the clergy to become another branch of the bureaucracy as their closeness to the peasantry rendered them suspect.[22] Religious observance was a significant part of the life of the Russian countryside. The rites connected with life's stepping-stones of birth, marriage and death were an integral part of peasant culture, even though they were often augmented by rituals which had their roots in ancient mythology, making peasant belief a rich mix of religion and superstition. Each peasant hut contained an icon and, while the theology of Orthodoxy might have been of no great interest to the peasantry, they did maintain a deep piety. The sense of community which was reinforced by Orthodoxy was replicated in groups which adhered to other religions. The Old Believers, a sect which had split from the Orthodox Church in the seventeenth century, numbered some ten million by 1905 and, partly as a result of persecution by the state, maintained a very powerful sense of identity. After 1905 and the greater tolerance which was shown to non-Orthodox religions, the Old Believers were able to hold regular congresses and to press forcefully for their rights as a community.[23] Russia was also rich in religious sects which rejected the Orthodox faith and practised a wide variety of rituals.

The Russian rural community was far from static. Peasants moved to and from the cities in search of work, but there was also migration from one rural area to another. The continuing expansion of the Russian Empire meant that there was a seemingly never-ending supply of lightly populated land available for settlement. Although much of the land in Siberia and Central Asia was inhospitable and migrating peasant families faced great hardships in establishing themselves, there was a continuous flow of migrants away from the densely populated provinces of central European Russia. At the end of the 1880s the government took steps to encourage migration by paying migrants' fares and giving financial assistance to help them set up new farms. This increased the rate of migration threefold so that 115 000 people moved each year between 1894 and 1903, and after the revolution of 1905 this flow of peasants grew yet further to reach more than 750 000 in 1908. The process of migration was important both in integrating the peripheral regions of the empire more closely into its overall fabric and in its impact on the rural environment of European Russia, even though a proportion of the settlers did find the experience too much for them and came home, reaching a peak in 1910 when 75 000 colonists made the return journey.[24]

The most dramatic evidence of migration in the Russian Empire was, however, in the growth of cities. In 1860 the urban population numbered just less than six million, but by 1914 it had risen to more than 18 million. Between 1863 and 1914 the population of the capital, St Petersburg, almost quadrupled to reach 2.1 million and the growth of Moscow was equally spectacular, with 1.75 million people living there in 1914. These two cities ranked fifth and seventh in the list of European cities by size in 1914, but there were 11 other Russian cities which by 1914 had a population of more than 100 000. The rate of growth of the urban population was more than twice that of the population as a whole, and much of this was accounted for by the great inflow of rural dwellers who came to seek work as the pace of industrialization quickened. By the 1880s more than 70 per cent of the population of the two greatest cities of the empire – St Petersburg and Moscow – was made up of immigrants who had been born elsewhere. Most of these people were peasants and their continued influx into the cities meant that in 1910 some 15 per cent of the Moscow population had lived in the city for less than one year. The urban population was, however, acquiring some degree of stability, since more than 5 per cent of the peasant population of both Moscow and St Petersburg had, by 1910, been living in the cities for over 20 years.

The rapidly expanding Russian cities had, therefore, widespread and close links with the rural environment which had produced most of their inhabitants. Immigrants to the cities usually maintained ties with their home villages and the village community continued to exert an influence on the urban environment through the efforts made by peasants in the cities to find work and housing for their fellows who had just arrived from their home village. Semen Kanatchikov, who went to work in Moscow from his village at the age of 18 in 1895, describes how the peasant patternmakers he worked with

> Would every payday without fail send part of their money back to the village . . . On holidays they attended mass and visited their countrymen and their conversations were mostly about grain, land, the harvest and livestock.[25]

Peasants from the same region would often work and live together. The chimney-sweeps of St Petersburg, for example, were overwhelmingly Finns and established this trade as one which successive generations of Finns entered.[26] The province of Tver was noted for providing Moscow with its stone-masons and Iaroslavl for waiters and shop assistants. A sense of community in the cities was also generated through cooperative forms of work organization which helped to moderate the dislocation that was the inevitable result of moving to the city. These informal associations of workers (*artels*) frequently rented communal apartments and were able, on the strength of their joint wages, to employ a woman to shop and cook for them. The 1897 census recorded 9 per cent of Moscow households and 6 per cent of St Petersburg households as living in communal, *artel*, arrangements.

For the Russian peasant immigrant to the city, becoming established as part of a group of people from the same region or in the same occupation was also a way of coping with the very difficult living conditions which confronted most urban workers. Housing was very crowded: in St Petersburg there were more than seven people to each apartment on average in 1900, and the situation was even worse in Moscow where in 1912 most of the population lived between two and four to a room. Public health was also poor. Stolypin spoke in the Duma in January 1911 in support of a government bill to introduce a sewerage scheme in St Petersburg, describing the Russian capital as a city

> Where one third of the deaths are caused by infectious diseases, where typhoid claims more victims than in any West European city, where smallpox is still rife, where recurrent typhus, a disease long eradicated in the West, is still occasionally seen and which is a favourite breeding ground for both cholera and plague bacteria.[27]

Although St Petersburg was recognized as being an especially unhealthy place to live, many other Russian cities were no better off when it came to sanitation and outbreaks of disease were common.

Although immigrants came to the cities primarily to work, the pattern of employment which they found was far from secure or stable. In many factories the whole labour force changed every year, right up to the first years of the twentieth century, and although employers tried to prevent such high labour turnover by retaining their workers' identity documents, this had only a limited impact in preventing workers' frequent changes of employment. It was not always easy, especially for unskilled workers, to obtain another job and a significant proportion of the populations of the biggest cities lived in extreme poverty. The numbers of the destitute were also swollen by those who were unable to work because of sickness or accident and by those who gravitated there with the intention of making some sort of living through begging. Some 350 000 of the population of Moscow were estimated to be in need at the beginning of the twentieth century.[28] Their existence, living in slums or in miserable lodging houses, able to secure only the most menial and short-term employment, was dispiriting. The responsibility for the welfare of the poor was largely in the hands of city councils from the 1890s onwards but the money available to alleviate suffering remained very limited.

Some workers sought to improve their lot, and that of their fellows, by combined action. Demands from urban workers for better conditions lay at the heart of the disturbances of 1905 and one of the concessions that the state made early in 1906 was to allow the formation of trade unions and workers' clubs. By the middle of 1907 more than 20 per cent of the St Petersburg factory labour force belonged to one of the 61 unions which had come into existence.[29] These new organizations were not strong enough to resist the renewed repression which was unleashed over the following five years as the government attempted to reassert its authority; by 1910 the unions in the capital could only count 5 per cent of factory workers as members. It took until 1912 for workers to acquire again the strength to act in unison when a renewed wave of protest took place, triggered by the killing of 200 workers by government troops. The demonstrators had gathered to present a petition to their employers in the Lena goldfields in Siberia. More than 350 000 workers went on strike during the year and urban protest intensified during the following 18 months, with the Factory Inspectorate recording 1.2 million workers striking in the first half of 1914. The strike movement was overwhelmingly concentrated in St Petersburg where over 45 per cent of strikers in 1914 were located and, with Riga and Moscow, accounted for more than 70 per cent of all strikers in the empire. This substantial level of activity by urban workers between 1912 and 1914 indicated a renewed sense of cohesion among the population of the largest cities of the Russian Empire.

Immigrants to the burgeoning cities of the empire were able to go some way towards recreating the sense of community which they had left behind in the countryside. Nevertheless, the social dislocation which many immigrants experienced was only partially assuaged by contact with their fellows who had moved to the city, whether through work or social contact. The sense of fracture with their old lives was emphasized by the difficult and unfamiliar living conditions, while the disciplines of factory work were as alien to Russian country people as they were to new workers right across Europe during the nineteenth century. It is not difficult to see why working people in the Russian Empire were attracted by organizations which offered some hope of ameliorating their lot. From 1912 onwards the influence of the Bolshevik party grew steadily in trade unions and other workers' organizations so that, as well as carrying out the legal functions of representation which these bodies possessed, Bolshevik-dominated trade unions became a cover for the dissemination of revolutionary propaganda and the organization of revolutionary protests. The process of urbanization and the social changes which it wrought produced an instability in Russian society which was equal to that in any other European society before 1914. The renewed conservatism of the Russian state in the years after 1905, and its refusal to act to improve the conditions of life for its workers, was in stark contrast to the social reforms enacted elsewhere in Europe in the years around 1900, and was vital in engendering a deep sense of discontent among Russia's urban workers.

Alongside the growth of this new social force, the traditional bulwark of the Russian state – the landed nobility – underwent a dramatic change in its role in the decades after emancipation. In 1863 there were more than 660 000 members of the hereditary nobility in European Russia, but they were far from being a homogeneous group. Immediately before emancipation, over three-quarters of the nobility owned less than 101 male serfs and only 1382 nobles possessed more than 1000 serfs. Many Russian nobles, especially those in the poorer agricultural regions, lived lives that were little better than those of the peasantry. At the other end of the scale, the great Russian noble families lived lives of great opulence, able to maintain houses in both country and city, to entertain extravagantly and to travel abroad. Land and agriculture were not, however, the only sources of the richer nobility's wealth and influence. Industry also contributed to their prosperity. The Bobrinskii family gained a very substantial income from their sugar refining businesses in the Ukraine while other nobles were able to exploit their ownership of forests to dominate the timber industry, and to use the grain which their estates produced to set up profitable distilleries. Nobles were also substantial property-owners in the growing cities, especially in St Petersburg and Moscow. The Sheremetev family owned particularly large urban estates in Moscow, letting nearly 50 buildings to businesses and making plans to build large blocks of apart-ments as well.[30]

It was land, however, which lay at the heart of the authority which the Russian nobility possessed. At emancipation, nobles owned nearly 80 million hectares of land in European Russia. The amount of land owned by the state and the imperial family exceeded this so that in physical terms the Russian lands were dominated by the state and its most faithful supporters. Before 1861 the nobility played a key role in maintaining order within the empire: their ownership of serfs gave them absolute authority over half the peasant population and the nobility exercised what were, in effect, police and judicial powers. The emancipation of the serfs in 1861 deprived the nobility of that formal authority and left them dependent on their land and on whatever offices individual nobles were able to acquire for themselves.

However, in the decades after emancipation the quantity of land owned by the nobility dropped inexorably. From 80 million hectares in 1861, it fell to 70 million in 1877 and to 47 million by 1905.[31] In 40 years the nobility divested themselves of 40 per cent of their land. By 1905 less than half of nobles belonged to landowning families. The reasons for this huge shift in the pattern of landholding stemmed from a common need for the Russian noble to adapt to a new environment, just as the peasantry had to do. Not all the nobility sold land; some nobles entered the land market to enhance their holdings and between 1863 and 1904 they purchased 42 million hectares. The market in noble-owned land was, therefore, extremely active as the nobility, themselves freed of their serfs, sought to make the adjustments to their landholdings that had been difficult to achieve before emancipation. Part of their motivation for sales of land was that many nobles were seriously in debt and needed to obtain the resources to put their financial situation on a more even keel. At least one-eighth of the money nobles gained from land sales went to pay off mortgages with the Nobles Land Bank. The rising price of land made this worthwhile, but even so the financial position of landowning nobles remained precarious and by 1905 more than 30 per cent of all noble landholdings were again mortgaged to the Land Bank.[32]

The difficulty of farming profitably in Russia affected the nobility as much as it did the peasantry, so some nobles took the opportunity to seek other methods of making a living. Leasing land to the emancipated peasantry was one option; by 1900 the peasantry was renting more than 60 per cent of all privately owned arable land. For many nobles, however, the solution to their difficulties was to abandon the land altogether as a source of income and to follow other occupations. Professional groups which expanded during the second half of the nineteenth century attracted nobles: in 1880 nearly one-fifth of Russian university professors were from the hereditary nobility. Fifteen per cent of Moscow nobles who supported themselves in the early 1880s were professional men.[33] Business was also an occupation which attracted the nobility: more than 700 nobles owned their own businesses in Moscow in 1882 and nearly 2500 were recorded in the municipal census that year as employed in commerce, transport or industry. The government bureaucracy had been the traditional, although not exclusive, preserve of the nobility and state service had also been a method of entry into the nobility: achievement of a senior rank in the civil service brought with it the conferment of nobility. As

87

reliance on the land, one pillar of the nobility's traditional role, declined, so nobles sought to strengthen their grip on the machinery of government. The Tsarist bureaucracy grew enormously in the half-century after emancipation, expanding more than threefold. But although the proportion of nobles staffing the government machine declined, so that in 1897 only 30 per cent of civil servants were noble, compared to more than 43 per cent during the 1850s, the absolute number of nobles who were able to gain employment as civil servants rose substantially. The 37 600 noble civil servants in 1857 had grown to more than 104 000 40 years later. The hereditary nobility succeeded in retaining a very powerful hold on the most senior posts in the empire, accounting for more than 1000 of the 1400 highest-ranking civil servants in 1897.[34] Emancipation therefore forced the Russian nobility to diversify and reduce their dependence on land. Although many landowners, especially those with small estates, found the going difficult and were forced to sell up, others reduced their landholding by choice and deliberately decided to follow another career.

Land and government service were not, however, the only ties which bound the nobility together. The nobility had developed a powerful sense of corporatism, expressed through formal organizations as well as through common attitudes. Each province and district of the empire had its own noble assembly which met each year to discuss matters of concern and to elect its leaders. These 'marshals of the nobility' were able to exercise very substantial power, if they were conscientious, through the network of official committees and boards on which they sat. The nobility were also well represented on the local councils (*zemstvo*) and both council chairmen and marshals of the nobility were regularly appointed to provincial governorships or vice-governorships by the government. The overt political role which the nobility played as a group was especially important in 1905 and during the following years. While many of those who pressed hard for political reform in the first years of the twentieth century were nobles, the overwhelming bulk of the nobility found themselves at odds with the process of change that was taking place in Russia. Provincial nobles felt especially threatened by calls in the First and Second Dumas for the expropriation of gentry land, and the nobility as a whole began to adopt a role which was explicitly political and which was aimed at defending its interests as a class. Since the late 1890s provincial marshals of the nobility had met as a group to discuss issues of concern and, after February 1905, they were able openly to debate political questions. At the end of November 1905 a conference of 203 landowners from 33 provinces gathered in Moscow and established the All-Russian Union of Land-owners.[35] This was an important step towards the creation of an organization which would represent all their interests and in May 1906 the first meeting of the United Nobility took place. The views which were put forward then and in successive conferences strongly endorsed the principle of private property and expressed doubts about the programme of reform which Stolypin's government had put forward.[36] The pressure which the United Nobility was able to exert after 1906 was significant in diverting the government from the path of reform and in reinforcing the conservatism of the regime. This influence was an important demonstration of the continued vigour of the nobility and their readiness to act to protect their traditional interests. Even though their involvement in land had declined, Russian provincial nobles were still extremely keen to preserve as much as possible of their traditional authority.

The development of industry, business and the professions in imperial Russia meant a considerable increase in the number of people who worked in these areas. In 1897 there were 17 000 doctors in the empire; by 1914 this figure had increased to over 28 000. Rural professions were also important: there were more than 5000 veterinary surgeons listed at the outbreak of war, and nearly 4000 qualified agronomists. The teaching profession grew substantially, the number of graduate teachers almost doubling between 1906 and 1914 to reach over 20 000.[37] Entrepreneurial skills were able to flourish in the late nineteenth-century climate which favoured industrialization: railway construction allowed men like Ivan Bliokh to rise from being a small contractor to heading the Southwestern Railway Corporation. On the Caspian Sea, the town of Baku saw the setting up of more than 80 petroleum refining companies during the early 1870s. By 1900 perhaps 2000 innovative and successful entrepreneurs had made a name for themselves in Russia.[38]

These middle groups in Russian society faced substantial difficulties in establishing themselves. The traditional legal structure of Russia was based on 'estate' organizations and recognized four groups – gentry, merchants, clergy and peasantry – as having particular privileges and duties. By the mid-nineteenth century this traditional model was beginning to lose its relevance as change swept through both rural and urban Russia. The state was only slowly coming to terms with Russian subjects whose occupation did not neatly fit into one of these four categories, or who were trying to move out of one estate group and into another. This did, in one way, intensify the need for the new professional and commercial groups to establish an identity as quickly as possible. They needed to find a forum to express concerns common to them as engineers, as sugar-producers, as lawyers and the like. They also faced the problem of social dislocation which was being experienced by the new Russian working class. These new business and professional men found the discontinuity in their lives eased by the lubricant of money and the opportunities which this gave them to create comfortable lives for themselves and their families. But the dislocation was nevertheless there for the noble's son who became a city lawyer or for the peasant who started his own textile business. Social need as much as the desire to defend commercial or professional interests pushed the middle groups in Russian society together.

These middle groups found various common threads in their lives which enabled them to begin the process of establishing a cohesive existence. Some elements were already there before emancipation and industrialization started to gnaw at the roots of Russian society: before 1850 the Old Believers, who had split from the Orthodox Church in the seventeenth century, had provided a core of industrialists. As their religious difference excluded them from the mainstream of Russian society, they had embarked on business careers and several Old Believer families had become extremely wealthy. The Riabushinskii family made their fortune through the Moscow cotton industry, as did the Morozovs, while in Nizhnii-Novgorod the Sirotkin family prospered from shipbuilding.

Other common elements developed as a result of the reform of the 1860s. The introduction of elected local councils meant, over the years, that a substantial number of professional people was needed to carry out the responsibilities which the councils possessed. By 1909 the 483 local councils employed more than 70 000 specialists. As well as doctors, teachers and vets they needed statisticians, pharmacists, insurance specialists, civil engineers and a host of managers to oversee the professional work of the council. These specialists came to identify themselves in two ways: as council employees and as members of their own profession on a national scale. Learned bodies had, of course, existed before the 1860s. The Imperial Russian Geographical Society, established in 1845, had provided a focal point for reformers in the 1850s, while the Free Economic Society had been founded in 1765 and the Academy of Sciences had existed since 1725. From the late 1860s onwards, professional associations and scientific societies flourished as forums were established for the exchange of ideas and experiences. The first All-Russian Teachers' Congress was held in 1872, the Pirogov Medical Society was set up in 1881 and the Moscow Legal Society was founded in 1863. Although the government deemed some of these organizations to be undesirable, such as the Congress of Council Statisticians, which met only once in 1887 before being prohibited, it was difficult to prevent the same individuals meeting under other guises – in 1894 the statisticians met instead as part of the Congress of Naturalists and Physicians.[39]

The numbers of voluntary organizations also mushroomed during the second half of the nineteenth century. Most Moscow clubs and societies before the 1860s were organizations dominated by and appealing to the nobility. By 1912, however, there were over 600 different associations in existence in the city. As well as the learned bodies which dealt with the serious issues of the day, a wide variety of leisure and sporting clubs catered for the interests of the middle ground in Russian society. The prosperous professional and business classes of the empire's cities amused themselves with the new technological marvels of the age: motor cars, aeroplanes and bicycles. Cycling clubs became so popular that in some parts of the empire the authorities took to issuing detailed regulations to ensure that cyclists could be properly identified.[40]

The public profile of middle groups in Russia grew steadily as the number of people involved in commerce and the professions increased. The corporate organizations which came into being to represent their interests could be vocal and insistent in their demands. Russian industrialists, in particular, could express their views forcibly: the Moscow section of the Russian Industrial Society frequently declared itself in favour of government measures to restrain Polish industry which it saw as dominated by German or Jewish interests.[41] In the 1860s textile manufacturers voiced their concerns about the high level of imports of finished cloth into the empire and the damaging effects that this was having on domestic industry. Industrial and commercial groups had established themselves to represent both particular industrial sectors and geographical concentrations of business. The St Petersburg Society of Factory and Mill Owners combined both functions, providing a voice for the capital's industrialists to express a coherent view, while it possessed different functional sections which allowed businessmen from the same industry to meet. It was only after 1905 that Russian industry organized itself on a national scale with the formation in 1906 of the Association of Industry and Trade. This body proved itself to have considerable political influence and had an important impact in getting a form of workers' insurance enacted by the Duma between 1908 and 1912. The significance of the business voice in the political life of the state had in any case been recognized by the government when the reform of the State Council in 1906 had resulted in the allocation of 12 seats to representatives of the industrial and commercial classes.

The cultural development of the empire was stimulated by middle groups in Russian society. The wealth which industry and commerce generated was partly used by well-off business and professional people to patronize the arts. The visual arts profited particularly from this approach and Moscow merchants provided a ready market for contemporary Russian paintings. Between 1871 and 1897 Pavel Tretiakov, who had made his fortune in the textile business, spent over one million rubles on buying works of art and his purchases came to form the nucleus of the Russian national collection of Russian art. The educated middle classes also bought books. Although serious literary journals – one of the main ways in which literature was published – had only a limited circulation before the 1880s, the market for the classics grew substantially, especially during the first years of the twentieth century. In 1913 more than 200 000 copies of Leo Tolstoi's books appeared in print along with over 100 000 copies of Gogol's works,[42] purchased mainly by the better off. The developing cultural tastes of the emerging Russian bourgeoisie helped to promote a degree of cohesiveness in terms of values and attitudes that was significant in creating a new middle force in Russian society.

The political achievements of the Russian middle classes were mixed. Although they could point to the granting of a form of constitution by Nicholas II in 1905 as representing the achievement in Russia of common European liberal demands for political reform, the work of the Duma itself proved to be a disappointment for the Russian bourgeoisie. Its failure to implement reform and the limited authority that the Duma could exercise demonstrated that the power of the traditional governing elite was still enormous. Although the new Russian middle groups did not succeed in gaining real political power, they did go a long way towards achieving social influence. The myriad of professional, commercial and recreational groups that came into being, particularly after 1905, were organizations which existed independently of both the autocratic state and of the traditional estate-based social structure of the empire. They represented potential challenges both to the domination of Russian society by the landed elites and to the state's exclusive hold on authority within the empire. The organizations to which the Russian middle classes belonged were largely autonomous of the state, as were the middle classes themselves. They did not depend on land for their prosperity and therefore possessed none of the ties to the state which land ownership had imposed on the nobility. Russian society was, in the decades after 1860, undergoing its most fundamental change as the more uniform estate structure was breaking down and being replaced by a much less homogeneous society. Diversity was much more difficult for the state to attempt to control and this, as much as the political changes which the empire underwent after 1905, posed a threat to the autocracy.

Other moves were afoot right through Russian society which served to increase the autonomy of individual Russians. The development of formal education and the concomitant growth of literacy were vital in allowing society to become more heterogeneous. Education for the mass of the empire's population was almost non-existent in the early 1860s. In 1856 the government educated nearly 433 000 pupils in a variety of schools controlled by different parts of the state bureaucracy. As the total population of the empire was then more than 70 million, a child's chances of obtaining education from the state were slim. This was not the only educational provision which existed, however, since the Orthodox Church played a significant part in schooling. In 1861 the Church reported that it controlled more than 9000 schools with a total of 159 000 pupils, although over the following 20 years more than half of its schools closed, leaving it with only 4000 in 1881. The emancipation of the serfs gave the freed peasantry the right to send their children to school, and this prompted a review of educational provision at all levels in the Russian Empire. Although an Education Statute was enacted in 1864, setting out the framework for primary education, the real drive to provide universal primary education only began during the 1890s. Russia's rapid moves towards industrialization meant that education was seen as vital to provide a capable workforce, while the need for agricultural innovation also pressed home the case for better schooling for the peasantry. Education was also seen by some as a means by which Russian society could be knitted together again and common values imparted to a population whose structure was changing rapidly.

Although the motives for encouraging the expansion of primary education were varied, they had a uniform effect. Direct central government spending on primary schools grew dramatically, increasing from five million rubles in 1896 to 19 million in 1907 and then to over 82 million rubles by the outbreak of war in 1914.[43] By 1911, over 6.5 million children aged between 8 and 11, 44 per cent of all children of that age, were receiving primary education in more than 100 000 schools. Educational provision was uneven: only one-third of pupils were girls; there were proportionately more schools in the Baltic provinces and in the central European regions of the empire and urban areas fared better than rural ones. The increased emphasis which the government placed upon improving access to education was matched by the enthusiasm with which the empire's population seized upon the opportunity. The provision of new schools and teachers could not, however, meet the demand for education which meant that a million children were unable to gain admission to a school in 1910.

The changes in Russian society from 1861 onwards meant that education became more and more valued. Urban workers often needed to be able to read and write to carry out their jobs effectively and the regular practice which they gained meant that they were able to develop their skills. An observer of sales staff in Odessa commented that 'their desire to acquire education and culture was slowly increasing. Gradually they were developing a sense of dignity and an awareness of their self-worth.'[44] For the peasantry too, education was of increasing value. The greater independence which emancipation provided in the 1860s for the individual peasant, as well as the substantial role which the commune acquired in self-government, made command of written language valuable for the rural dweller.

While primary education in Russia was taking steps towards universal provision, secondary and higher education remained much more the preserve of social elites. Successive ministers pursued policies which tinkered with the curriculum, but the government maintained at heart the view that was most forcibly expressed in the notorious comment by Ivan Delianov in 1887, while he was Minister of Education, that secondary schools should not provide for 'children of coachmen, servants, cooks, washerwomen, small shopkeepers and persons of a similar type'.[45] Although in 1911 one-quarter of students in secondary schools came from the peasantry, this represented only some 30 000 individuals. In 1897 one-quarter of the nobility had received some form of secondary schooling, but only one-tenth of 1 per cent of peasants. Higher education was viewed with especial wariness by the government because universities were believed to be a breeding-ground for revolutionary opinions. The conservative journalist Mikhail Katkov, writing in 1879, argued that

The state cannot let education slip out of its hands ... Education cannot be left to the chance whim or biases of men without responsibility... If the grammar schools provide students for the universities, so the universities provide the grammar schools with teachers – and the state with all manner of officials.[46]

The number of students studying at Russian universities grew fourfold in the 35 years after 1865, but still only reached 16 000 by 1900. The paternalistic authoritarianism of the government was shaken in its dealings with universities, as in so many other areas, by the revolution of 1905 and student numbers grew from 21 000 in 1904 to a peak of over 38 000 five years later. This increase was matched by the growth of student numbers at technical institutes.[47]

The expansion of formal education had important consequences. The empire-wide census of 1897 gave the first comprehensive picture of literacy rates, indicating that 21 per cent of the entire population were literate. This concealed huge disparities between different social groups: rural literacy remained low at 17 per cent while 45 per cent of urban dwellers were literate. More men – 29 per cent – were literate than women – 13 per cent, but the divide here between city and country was even more pronounced as only 9 per cent of rural women could read and write, as opposed to 35 per cent of their urban counterparts. Industrial workers had an especially high level of literacy. Two-thirds of male metal-workers were literate, and more than half of all workers could read and write.[48] Literacy had been rising during the nineteenth century: between 1874 and 1904 the literacy of army recruits had increased from 21 per cent to 55 per cent. The process quickened after 1900: by 1913 30 per cent of the entire population was literate and, if children below school age are excluded from the figures, this rises to 38 per cent. Tsarist education played an important role in this process. The last generation to graduate from the empire's schools were between 12 and 16 when the 1920 census was taken: 71 per cent of boys and 52 per cent of girls in that age group were then literate.

Literacy meant that individual Russians could form their own response to the wide range of written materials that were becoming available in the empire. In 1855 only 1239 editions of books were published in the Russian Empire, rising by 1895 to 11 548 editions printed in more than 42 million copies. In the following 20 years, the volume of books increased three-fold to reach more than 32 000 titles in 130 million copies. By 1900, more than 600 periodicals were being published in Russian and after 1905 the quantity of newspapers increased significantly so that 1767 appeared at least weekly in 1914.[49] A substantial proportion of this printed output was directed at the ordinary reader, often those who were newly literate, and the establishment of reading rooms by philanthropic individuals and organizations helped to make the printed word accessible for them. Much of the content of books and periodicals was concerned with rural themes which would be of interest to the peasant, either still resident in the countryside or else one of the migrants to the towns. Alongside this, popular literature propounded the values of the newly industrializing society. Success was usually portrayed as available in the urban environment, sometimes simply from a job in the city, or else from the ownership of a small business. The models which popular writing presented to readers were of people who had worked to develop their own talents and had been able to achieve success through their efforts, albeit often tempered with a great deal of good luck.

Literacy also opened the doors to other types of writing. The writer Maxim Gorkii, born the son of a carpenter, described in his autobiography *My Universities* how in the 1880s his ability to read meant that he was able to read and study the works of John Stuart Mill, as well as to join circles which debated the ideas in prohibited books by Russian radicals such as Peter Lavrov and Nikolai Chernyshevskii. While radical political and social ideas could be disseminated in imperial Russia through the clandestine circulation of works which were prohibited by the censor, imaginative literature also played a crucial role in this process. Many prominent Russian writers and artists believed that their duty was not to produce 'art for art's sake', but to use their work to deal with the concrete problems which they perceived in Russian society. The novelist Mikhail Saltykov-Shchedrin wrote that

> Literature and propaganda are the same thing . . . Fiction does not give the reader that totality and certainty of knowledge which science leads to . . . but its influence can all the same be beneficial in that it is predisposed to searching for truth and makes the reader approach sceptically those unconscious axioms which he has been guided by up to then.[50]

Art was a serious matter and, especially in the years before 1905, the responsibility which Russian writers and artists felt towards their society resulted in realist works which reflected a tendentious approach. This was defined by Vladimir Stasov, an influential critic, as art 'which has the force of indignation and accusation, which is filled with protest and a passionate desire to destroy everything which oppresses and burdens the world'.[51] This approach was reflected in some of the great novels which appeared during the 1860s and 1870s. Leo Tolstoi published *War and Peace* in 1869 and *Anna Karenina* between 1875 and 1877 while Fedor Dostoievskii wrote *Crime and Punishment* in 1866, following this in the subsequent 15 years with *The Idiot* and *The Brothers Karamazov*. Anton Chekhov's stories and plays which appeared from the 1880s until his death in 1904 continued the tradition of realist writing which dealt with both contemporary problems and matters of universal significance. By the beginning of the twentieth century works of serious literature were appearing in cheap, mass-produced editions which made them accessible to many of the newly literate, as well as to the educated elites who had formed their initial audience. This approach was not limited to the written word, as from 1870 a group of painters mounted travelling exhibitions which displayed their works of realist art. These *Itinerants*, setting themselves up in conscious opposition to the sterile academic traditions which had predominated in Russian art, produced paintings which depicted the life of ordinary people, as well as realist portrayals of the more traditional subjects of the artist's brush. Their paintings, by artists such as Ilia Repin, Isaac Levitan and Ivan Kramskoi, dealt with topics such as the effects of urbanization and the problems faced by the peasantry after emancipation.

The social impact of this type of art was considerable. Some of the *Itinerants'* paintings were prohibited from public exhibition by the government, while the continuing outpourings of literature, by lesser names as well as the great Russian writers, ensured that discussion of important social questions continued, despite the government's attempts at censorship. The relaxation of controls on expression which took place after 1905 did have some impact on the literature that was produced: the 'Silver Age' of Russian culture, as the ten years or so before 1917 were known, was dominated more by poets who saw much less need to address social questions in their art and, instead, concentrated on experimenting with form and on dealing with the universal subjects of art. Writers such as Anna Akhmatova, Alexander Blok and Osip Mandelshtam all found fame though this approach. Russian culture displayed great originality and vitality in the first years of the twentieth century. The Futurist manifesto drawn up by the poets Vladimir Maiakovskii and Viktor Khlebnikov in 1912 was entitled 'A Slap in the Face of Public Taste'; Igor Stravinsky's music shocked European high society while Diaghilev's dancers revolutionized the world of ballet. The visual arts were also part of this cultural upheaval: Chagall's pictures and Malevich's dramatic Suprematist paintings played a major role in the development of European abstract art. By the beginning of the First World War, Russian culture was diverse and cultural manifestations which had previously been the preserve of the highly educated elite were becoming more widely disseminated among the population of the empire.

This trend was indicative of the changes which ran through Russian society after 1855. Russian subjects were increasingly able to draw on sources of knowledge and support which were independent of the Tsarist regime. The old certainties of Russian society – the dominance of the landed nobility and their explicit control over the peasantry – were destroyed by emancipation. The hold which the peasant commune could exert over its members was much looser than the ties which had bound serf to lord, and the rapid growth of factories and the accompanying process of urbanization was a further factor which served to unknit rural society. As more people went to live in towns, so they were exposed to new and different influences, shaped by the world of disciplined work which now dominated their lives. The close ties which migrants maintained with their home villages meant that rural society gradually became exposed to the ideas and values which industrialization brought. Even though peasant Russia might reject such ideas, every village had its contingent of inhabitants who worked in towns and returned to recount the experiences they had there. Russian society was fragmenting in the 60 years after 1855: the traditional rural relationship between lord and master was broken by emancipation and, as the nobility ran down their landholdings, any moral authority which they may have held decreased. Urban workers and the new urban middle classes existed only fitfully as coherent groups, and although bonds were growing inside urban society, by 1914 neither worker nor businessman could claim to be part of a unified group.

Diversity and autonomy were therefore becoming important characteristics of Russian society. Education meant that the newly literate could absorb information and opinion much more easily: the imperial regime could not hope to control effectively the ideas to which its population was exposed. Even though change came only slowly to the lives of the

100 million peasants of the empire, by 1914 the dynamics of Russian society were moving at a pace which the state could no longer regulate. The old social order had irretrievably broken down but a new equilibrium had not yet been reached.

4

EMPIRE AND EUROPE

The Russian Empire was the largest state on earth, stretching from the Prussian border in the west to the Pacific Ocean in the east, from the icy Arctic northern coast to the Chinese border. The empire was inhabited by more than 100 different ethnic groups. The Slav peoples of Russia, Ukraine and Belorussia made up more than two-thirds of the population, but huge variety of minority groups, ranging from Finns in the north-west to Kazakhs in Central Asia, meant that it was never an easy task to govern such a disparate collection of peoples. Language, religion and cultural traditions all varied dramatically across the Russian state. The Russian domains differed from other European-centred empires in one critical respect: Russian conquerors had never had to go *overseas* to acquire their Empire. The Russian Empire was amassed by expansion into territory which was contiguous to Russia's existing possessions, resulting in continual challenges to integrate ethnically and economically diverse regions into the main body of the state.

Like that of other European Great Powers, Russian imperial expansion was brisk during the second half of the nineteenth century. Russian territorial expansion, as much as that of other states, exacerbated existing international rivalries and created new tensions, sharpened in Russia's case by the fact that its imperial expansion was simultaneously an extension of the Russian state itself across the Eurasian land mass. Since the mid-eighteenth century Russia had been gradually expanding its control over Central Asia between the Caspian Sea in the west and the Chinese state to the east. The independent states of the region fell to Russia one by one. By 1850 the three Kazakh Hordes occupying the lands south of Cheliabinsk and Omsk – numbering about 1.5 million people in total – had been subjugated and the Russians then turned their attention to the Uzbek territories further south. Prince Alexander Gorchakov, Foreign Minister between 1856 and 1882, described Russia's situation in Central Asia as being

> the same as the position of any civilized state which comes into contact with a semi-barbarous people . . . In such cases the interests of frontier security and of trade relations always require that the more civilized state acquires a certain power over its neighbours.[1]

Russian troops advanced steadily south from 1850 onwards, annexing large areas of the Uzbek lands in the mid-1850s and conquering the city of Tashkent in 1865. Kokand became a Russian protectorate in 1868 and was formally annexed to the empire eight years later. The khanates of Bokhara and Khiva fell in 1868 and 1873 respectively and after the newly acquired lands had been incorporated into the Governor-Generalship of Turkestan, centred on Tashkent, the remote desert and mountain areas of the Kara-Kum and the Pamirs were taken during the 1880s and 1890s. By 1895 Russia's southern border touched Persia and Afghanistan and was, from the British point of view, perilously close to India. Russia's Central Asian conquests posed it relatively few problems: Russian military might was able to subdue the peoples of the region without facing any opposition that seriously threatened to delay its progress.

The situation was rather different in the Far East, the second region in which Russia was able to consolidate its power after 1850. The growth of Russia's power in this area brought it up against the Chinese state and Russian expansion was assisted by the difficulties in which China found itself at the end of the 1850s. With Britain and France at war with China between 1856 and 1858, Nikolai Muravev, Governor-General of Eastern Siberia, was able to press home the advantages he had made since his appointment in 1847. Expeditions were sent down the River Amur in 1854, 1855 and 1857 and Muravev established a new administrative region, the Maritime District, to act as a bridgehead for Russia's advance to establish itself firmly on the Pacific coast and thus acquire a further outlet to the sea. Russians reached what was to become Vladivostok in 1859. The following year the Chinese had to concede the loss of significant areas of territory which allowed the Russian Empire access to the Sea of Japan. This did not, however, bring the Far East to the fore of the St Petersburg government's thinking. Central Asian expansion took priority in the 1860s and 1870s as the Far East appeared to provide less opportunity for Russia to demonstrate its potency in relation to other Great Powers. The sheer distance of the Far Eastern region from Russia's heartland and the difficulty of communication also made it a less attractive immediate focus of attention.

The impetus which Muravev had given to the Far Eastern adventure slackened after 1860. In 1867 Russia sold Alaska to the United States and less than ten years later allowed Japan to take control of the northern part of the Kurile island chain in exchange for the entire island of Sakhalin. It was not until the 1890s that Russia's imperial ambition again focused on the Pacific region. The initiation of the construction of the Trans-Siberian railway in 1891 gave the promise of improved links between the Far East and European Russia which would allow the St Petersburg government to implement policy effectively in a region some 10 000 km away. Sergei Witte, in particular, believed that Russia should become a great Eastern power and that the weakness of China provided the opportunity for the extension of Russian influence, especially in Manchuria. Following China's defeat in war with Japan in 1894, the Li-Lobanov treaty of 1896 gave Russia the right to build the Chinese Eastern Railway across northern Manchuria and in 1898 Russia was able to extract Chinese agreement to Russia's leasing of the Liaotung peninsula. With this came the building of a Russian naval base at Port Arthur on the Yellow Sea and the construction of a railway to link the new base to the Eastern railway at Harbin.

The motivation for Russian imperial growth was deep-seated. Since the sixteenth century and the beginnings of the great expansion of the Muscovite city-state, the Russian state had increased its domains by a continual process of acquiring and developing adjacent territories. In Europe this had brought it possession of large areas of Poland at the end of the eighteenth century and of Finland in 1808, while movement east and south into Asia was a gradual and continuing process. The lack of natural physical barriers to Russian expansion, together with the lack of powerful opposition, meant that the Russian Empire faced no great difficulties, other than those of climate and terrain, in moving east and south to annex Asian lands. Russian movement into the Caucasus, however, had met with substantial armed opposition and the Russian army was constantly involved in fighting in the region during the 1830s and 1840s. Some of the motivation for territorial expansion was to guarantee the political security of the Russian state. But the lack of natural barriers to Russian territorial growth also posed a potential threat: aggressors could take advantage of the same ease of movement to launch attacks on Russian territory. The example of the Tatar domination of Russia from the thirteenth century until their influence was finally thrown off by Ivan III two centuries later remained an important part of the Russian political psyche. Consequently, as Russia moved into new areas, there was a need to protect the new borderlands and hence a continuing imperative to expand further and further.

Alongside this desire to protect Russia's security there were also important economic reasons for the acquisition of more territory. The rich resources of Siberia had acted as a powerful magnet for Russian explorers during the sixteenth and seventeenth centuries, drawing fur traders in particular to the colder areas of northern Asia where fur-bearing animals could be trapped. Once expeditions into the expanses of Siberia had uncovered some of the other natural riches which existed there, the minerals and timber became increasing targets for exploitation. The economic wealth of the lands which bordered the Russian state and the opportunities which they offered to commerce reinforced the political desire to expand. Furthermore, the lands of Siberia and Central Asia provided trade between Russia, China and other Asian states. Political control of these lands therefore became crucial for Russia.

During the second part of the nineteenth century Russia's imperial expansion was closely linked to the manoeuvres of the Great Powers in Asia. The rivalries of the European states were largely played out in lands outside Europe. Russia's defeat in the Crimean War between 1854 and 1856, made all the more embarrassing because it was a defeat sustained on Russia's own territory, left it with considerable resentment towards the victorious states of France and Britain. The British possessions in India provided a potential target for the more gung-ho Russian generals and publicists who wanted to see Russia exact some form of revenge for the Crimean defeat and who favoured rapid expansion in Central Asia so that the British position there could be challenged. In both London and India, British authorities perceived a threat to Britain's position from the rapid Russian advance southwards, and this encouraged Britain to strengthen its own position in the states which acted as 'buffers' between British India and the Russian Empire. Persia, Afghanistan and Tibet all found themselves the object of even more intense attention.

Growing British interest in these areas appeared threatening to Russia's new dominions, still inadequately integrated into the empire, and this in its turn motivated Russia to expand to protect its dominions.

Similar pressures were at work in the Far East. The decline of the Chinese state presented opportunities for European powers other than Russia to make their mark in the region. In 1897 Germany took possession of the Chinese port of Kiaochow (Tsingtao) and in the following year the British demanded that China lease them the port of Wei-hai-wei. The French acquired a base in Kwangchow Bay in 1898 while the existing British possession of Hong Kong and the Portuguese settlement at Macao provided further evidence of European powers' interest in the Far East. As each of the Great Powers attempted to stake a claim for a part of the disintegrating Chinese empire, Russia clearly felt compelled to join in the process. The political balance was further complicated by the emergence of Japan as a substantial regional power. Japanese strength was made even more alarming to Russia by the 1902 alliance between Britain and Japan: Britain recognized Japan's special interest in Korea and agreed to keep France neutral, despite the 1894 Franco-Russian alliance, should a war break out between Russia and Japan. Even though advancing into the Far East was difficult and expensive for the Russian state, the interest which was being displayed in the region by other Great Powers meant that Russia could not afford to stand back and watch its rivals gain territory and influence on its eastern doorstep. International considerations, more than any pressing domestic concerns, lay at the heart of Russian imperial expansion.

The results of expansion were not always wholly beneficial for Russia. Bringing more territories under Russian control meant that the ethnic and religious composition of the empire became even more diverse. The conquest of substantial areas of Central Asia brought great numbers of Muslims into the empire: by 1900 the Muslim population numbered 10 million. The needs of the Russian state could conflict with the different culture and traditions which the Muslims possessed. Although in 1867 the military governor of Turkestan had recognized that 'the centuries-old structure of the Muslim states cannot be transformed into a European pattern by any persuasion, advice or threats from Russia',[2] the growing influx of Russian migrants to the region had its effects. There were a number of small uprisings after 1880, but the Russian administration failed to recognize the signs of alarm among the Muslim population at Russian cultural and economic imperialism. Central Asian Muslims were able to take advantage of the greater freedom of expression available after 1905 by making representations about their religious freedom and the security of the Muslim economy of the region. The impact of the First World War in Central Asia proved, however, to be dramatic, even though there was no foreign enemy in the area. In 1916 there was a mass revolt by Muslims protesting against the imposition of conscription in Central Asia. This resulted in the killing of over 3250 Russians and of many more Muslims as the army put down the uprising with great severity.[3] Tensions were less obvious in the Far Eastern lands which the Russians acquired. The population was much smaller and very sparsely distributed while the number of Russians who moved into the area was also small.

These problems of imperial expansion mirrored the existing situation within the empire. Less than 20 miles from St Petersburg, the proximity of Finland – where many of the capital's elite had summer houses – continually reminded ministers and officials of the heterogeneity of the state. Along the southern shore of the Baltic Sea, Estonians, Latvians and Lithuanians spoke their own distinctive languages, while the landowning nobility of the region were mainly German in origin. Travelling to Western Europe from St Petersburg usually meant journeying through Russia's Polish domains where the majority of the empire's Jewish population lived. While the Russian state traced its own roots back to the city of Kiev in the ninth century, Kiev was claimed by Ukrainian nationalists as the centre of a distinct Ukrainian nation. More than a million Romanians lived in Bessarabia in the south-west of the empire, while in the Caucasus territorial acquisitions in the 70 years after 1783 had brought Georgians and Azerbaijanis into the empire, together with a multitude of smaller national groups.

The way in which the St Petersburg government dealt with the non-Russian groups inside the empire changed during the second half of the nineteenth century. Although the Russian state had reacted with severity to events such as the Polish uprising of 1830, national minorities had generally given the government only little cause for concern before 1850. The development of nationalist ideology during the nineteenth century did not, however, leave the Russian Empire untouched. In those areas where there was already a developed and separate national culture, such as Poland and Finland, the ideology of national self-determination found a ready audience. Even the severe measures which the Russian government took to quell Polish nationalism after the great rebellion of 1863 failed, and by the 1880s a modern and cohesive nationalist movement had come into being. A nationalist journal, *Glos* (The Voice), was established in Warsaw in 1886, and called for mass political action to counter Russian rule; the Union of Polish Youth came into existence the following year as a radical student organization.[4] In Finland, a student association to advance the Finnish language had been set up in 1847 and nationalist pressure meant that in 1886 Finnish was recognized by the Russian government as an official language in Finland.[5] The growth of national sentiment was not confined to regions of the empire which had a history of recent independence. As elsewhere in Europe, national groups which had previously been quiescent began to find a voice and to assert their identity as a distinct group which deserved distinct rights. In the Ukraine the secret Brotherhood of Saints Cyril and Methodius, devoted to awakening a national consciousness among Ukrainians, came into being in the 1840s and survived until its discovery by the police in 1847. There was renewed activity among Ukrainians in the 1860s with the establishment in 1861 of the first Ukrainian journal in the empire and a move to set up a network of Sunday schools around Kiev for the peasantry. The aftermath of the Polish uprising of 1863, however, drew renewed antagonism from the imperial authorities and the St Petersburg government prohibited the publication of any item in the Ukrainian language which was of a scholarly, religious or educational nature. The imperial Minister of Internal Affairs, Peter Valuev, wrote that the Ukrainian language 'never existed, does not exist and never shall exist'.[6] Tentative contacts were made between Ukrainian nationalists and the Populist movement in the 1870s and during the 1890s both Ukrainian liberal and socialist political parties came to articulate explicitly nationalist goals.

The peoples of the Baltic provinces also began to express their own national aspirations. Estonian culture began to come into its own: two Estonian newspapers were founded in 1856, an Estonian school movement was established during the 1860s and the first of what was to become the most significant expression of Estonian nationhood – the All-Estonian Song Festival – was held in 1869. The same process was taking place among the Latvians. Newspapers and periodicals began to be published in quantity in Latvian during the 1860s and the Riga Latvian Association was established in 1868, initially to support the activities of the Latvian middle classes but later to act as a means of consolidating the national aspirations of the Latvian people as a whole. Sentiment in the Baltic provinces was directed against two groups. First, from the 1880s onwards the Russian state attempted to increase central control over the Baltic provinces and was thus was an obvious target for nationalist activists. Second, the position was complicated by the German elite which dominated both the economy and the political life of the region through its landholdings and the power which they conferred. Tensions between the German population and the Estonians and Latvians were of long standing and were heightened by the developing national identities of the Baltic peoples.

The Baltic Germans held on to administrative and judicial authority in the region through the noble corporations which united them. German-language education was provided both in schools and by a German university in Tartu (Dorpat). The Lutheran religion also acted as a cohesive force for the German population, despite the growing activity of the Orthodox Church in missionary work among the peasant population of the region. The 125 000 or so Baltic Germans occupied an exceptional place in the Russian Empire since they provided a disproportionate number of the state's most senior civil servants. Despite belonging to a national minority with its roots in a different language and religion, more than 10 per cent of the men appointed to the State Council between 1894 and 1914 were of Baltic German ancestry.[7] Tensions existed in the Baltic region between the German elite and the largely peasant indigenous population. The peasantry resented the power of their largely German masters and this became an important component of the nationalist awakening in the Baltic provinces of the empire. The Baltic Germans were also viewed increasingly with suspicion by Russian nationalists. Conservative thinkers such as Iurii Samarin and Mikhail Pogodin argued during the 1860s and 1870s that Baltic German influence was too strong and that the Baltic provinces should be more closely integrated into the overall structures of the Russian Empire. The Baltic provinces therefore found themselves in a situation of deep social division along national lines; landowner was pitted against peasant and both found the attentions of Russian nationalists to be uncongenial.

This process of national awakening was taking place right across the Russian Empire. German colonists had been encouraged to settle in the interior of the Russian Empire in the mid-eighteenth and early nineteenth centuries and had established themselves largely along the Lower Volga and in southern Ukraine. By 1912 there were nearly half a million Volga Germans who spoke their own dialect of German, held fast to Lutheranism or Catholicism despite being in the midst of a sea of Orthodox believers, and nurtured a culture which was very different from that of their Russian neighbours. The upheavals of 1905 provided the impetus for the development of the Volga Germans' cohesion: they were able to begin to publish their own newspapers and, in particular, to express their unhappiness with the government's insistence on the use of the Russian language in their schools.[8] The arrest of a prominent Volga German activist in the summer of 1906 provoked serious disturbances, as the normally quiescent population of the region's principal town rose against the Russian authorities.

There were other distinct groups in the empire where discontent was more explicable. The Jewish population was a particular target of discrimination. The successive partitions of Poland at the end of the eighteenth century had substantially increased the number of Jews under the jurisdiction of the Russian Empire, so that by 1897 they numbered about five million. They were restricted to living in a limited area of the empire – the Polish provinces and the south and west of European Russia itself – and were a distinctive group, possessing their own language and religion as well as having a far smaller involvement in agriculture than the majority of the people around them. Jews had their choice of employment severely restricted, since government service was almost entirely closed to them and specific limits were imposed on access to education in 1887. In the Jewish Pale of Settlement, only 10 per cent of the students in secondary and higher education could come from the Jewish population, a proportion which was reduced to 5 per cent for the remainder of the empire, except in St Petersburg and Moscow where only 3 per cent of such students could be Jews. The imposition of these quotas, more than anything else, served to disillusion young Jews and to make them recognize that they would have grave difficulty in improving themselves under the Tsarist regime. This discontent was fuelled by the frequent recurrence of violent attacks on Jews and their communities – pogroms – which were at times officially sponsored and to which the Tsarist authorities often turned a blind eye. In these circumstances, it is not surprising that revolutionary political groups found it easy to recruit Jewish adherents or that, once political groups could be legally established in 1905, a liberal Jewish party – the Union for the Attainment of Full Equality for the Jewish People – came into being.[9]

The multinational nature of the empire thus presented the imperial government with substantial challenges, but the response of St Petersburg to national minorities was confused and inconsistent. The government had no coordinating body which dealt with national questions and it confronted problems which arose case by case, rather than systematically. At the same time, the government was assailed by differing pressures which pushed it in varying directions. The intensification of nationalist ideology which provoked some of the smaller national groups inside the empire to assert their own identity also had an impact on Russians themselves. Renewed emphasis on the virtues of the Slav peoples and on the particular place which they had to play in history led a series of thinkers and publicists to emphasize the Russianness of the empire. The philosopher Nikolai Danilevskii stressed the differences between Russia and other European nations and called for 'exclusivity and patriotic fanaticism' in dealing with Western influences.[10] Mikhail Katkov, who as the editor of two journals – *The Russian Messenger* and *Moscow News* – during the 1870s and 1880s gained a considerable following, argued that Russia should be a homogeneous state and that other national claims within the empire were inadmissible. He wrote in 1865 that

We do not want coercion or persecution or constraints against ethnic peculiarities, dialects and languages, or still less against the religious conscience of non-Russians; but we do indeed propose that the Russian government can be solely Russian throughout the whole expanse of the possessions of the Russian power, which have been gained by Russian blood.[11]

This view which encapsulated the idea that Russianness and Russian values should be extended right across the Russian empire, rather than just being confined to the native Russian population, became an important element in the thinking of the government with the accession to the throne of Alexander III in 1881.

The attitudes which the state displayed towards national minorities were closely aligned with its overall political direction, and the changes in political thinking that took place after 1855 help to explain the radical shifts in policy towards non-Russian groups. Control always rested at the heart of the Russian government's concerns and even though reform was the centrepiece of Alexander II's policy during the 1860s, the government acted decisively to put down the Polish rebellion of 1863. The rising consisted mainly of guerrilla fighting against the Russians. It involved more than 200 000 Poles altogether and brought with it the formation of an underground National Government for Poland, but was suppressed by Russian armies under the Viceroy, Grand Duke Konstantin Nikolaevich, the Tsar's brother.

While military force was used to suppress Polish national aspirations, Alexander II used other methods elsewhere in the empire to attempt to secure effective control. In the Baltic provinces, decisions taken in 1864 and 1875 allowed some 35 000 Estonians and Latvians to revert to Lutheranism following the coercive policies previously pursued to promote the Orthodox Church.[12] The Finns were also treated with some sympathy by Alexander II. Finland was unique in the Russian Empire before 1905 as it possessed a form of parliament, inherited when Sweden ceded Finland to Russia in 1809. Alexander II called what was only the second meeting of the Diet since Russia's acquisition of Finland and, in his speech at its opening in 1863, he declared that he wanted to see an accord between the Finnish people and their sovereign. He went on

> [This] will be of great assistance to the well-being of this region, so close to my heart ... You, representatives of the Grand Duchy, must prove by your work, fidelity and composure in decisions, that in the hands of a wise people, ready to act as one with the Sovereign, with practical ideas for the development of their welfare, liberal institutions are not only not dangerous, but are a guarantee of order and prosperity.[13]

The good relations that existed between the Finns and the imperial government in the 1860s and 1870s are confirmed by the continuing existence of one of the few statues of Alexander II in the centre of Helsinki.

The move away from reform at the beginning of the 1880s was reflected in the attitudes which the government displayed towards non-Russian nationalities. As part of the attempts which the imperial authorities made to increase their direct control over the population, national groups found that the St Petersburg government implemented a variety of policies which sought to affirm the Russian nature of the empire during the 1880s and 1890s. Reducing the heterogeneity of the state would serve to buttress the Tsarist regime: General Nicholas Bobrikov, on taking up his appointment as Governor-General of Finland in 1898, declared that

> Russia is one and indivisible ... Throughout the whole vast territory of Russia all who are subjects under the mighty sceptre of the Tsar must know themselves to be of one realm and share the love for a common fatherland.[14]

External manifestations of nationality increasingly found disapproval with the imperial government. Use of the Ukrainian language in publications or public performances was completely prohibited in 1876, while at the same time the government resolved to offer financial support to a newspaper which was openly hostile to Ukrainian national ambitions.[15] The state rarely went so far as to totally forbid the public use of a language, recognizing that such a policy was extremely difficult to enforce, but it did put great pressures on the non-Russian population of the empire to become accustomed to utilizing Russian, rather than their native language, in their everyday lives. In Poland the Russian state sought to promote assimilation in the wake of the 1863 rebellion by insisting on the use of Russian in the courts and in local government. Russian became the language of local administration in the Baltic provinces in 1885, and Baltic legal reform in 1888 and 1889 brought with it the compulsory use of Russian in the higher courts. These reforms did not, however, affect the self-governing institutions controlled by the Baltic German landowners; they remained immune from this process of linguistic imperialism and continued to conduct their business in German. In Finland, the use of Russian for administrative matters was also greatly extended by the Language Edict of 1900. The Finnish Senate, which dealt with justice and with the administration of Finland, was to conduct all its business with the Governor-General – the representative of the imperial government – in Russian, and provincial administrations were to operate in Russian when dealing with central bodies.

Alongside the use of Russian in administrative matters came a greater insistence on its place in education right across the empire. In Poland the native tongue could only be taught as a foreign language, so that Polish children had to use Russian when learning their own language at school. The Ukrainian language edict laid down that primary schools could not teach in Ukrainian – or Little Russian as the edict termed the Ukrainian language. It was also suggested that teachers who had been trained in the Ukrainian provinces should be appointed to teaching posts in regions far from their homes and that schools in Ukraine should be staffed by teachers from the Russian heartland. The imperial government regarded institutions of higher education in non-Russian areas with particular suspicion. It was all too aware of the role which universities had played in developing opposition to the state and did not wish to see this process accentuated in non-Russian areas by the addition of nationalist ideology to the already potent brew which was producing the nascent socialist movement in the 1880s and 1890s. This was one area in which the imperial government did act to restrict the privileges of the Baltic Germans: the German-speaking university in Tartu was compelled to provide instruction in Russian between 1889 and 1895 and the city itself lost its German name of Dorpat and instead received the Russian name of Iurev. In Finland, plans were made to institute new professorships in Russian law and Russian history at the Alexander University in Helsinki and for these topics to be taught in Russian. Action had already been taken in the wake of the Polish rebellion to establish a new Russian-language university in Warsaw in 1869.

Religious affiliation was also a clear symbol of national identity where the Tsarist regime sought to intensify the homogeneity of the empire. As well as providing encouragement to the Orthodox Church to proselytize amongst adherents to other religions, the government also took steps to make the Orthodox religion more attractive to others. In the Baltic provinces, land was provided for landless Orthodox peasants and financial support was made available to improve the quantity of Orthodox-controlled schools. During the 13 years of Alexander III's reign, it is estimated that 37 000 Lutherans in the Baltic region underwent conversion to Orthodoxy, although some returned to Lutheranism when religious toleration was increased after 1905. The Roman Catholic religion had suffered in the 1860s as the imperial government tried to break its ties with Polish nationalism. Catholic monasteries in Poland were closed down, the influence of Catholic priests was curbed and incentives were provided to encourage non-Catholics to buy land in Poland. As the Russian Empire expanded into the Far East and Central Asia, intense activity took place to promote Orthodoxy. The All-Russian Orthodox Missionary Society was established in 1870 and by 1894 it was able to proclaim that nearly 60 000 'heathens and Muslims' had become Orthodox as a result of its work. A visit by the future Nicholas II to Siberia in 1891 provided the excuse for the forced mass baptism of members of the Buriat community.[16]

These visible expressions of nationality were not the only targets of the imperial government in attempting to extend the Russian nature of the state to all its component parts. The imperial army was seen as an effective method of promoting uniformity amongst the different peoples of the empire by inculcating Russianness into new conscripts. In 1901 the separate Finnish army was abolished and Finns were made liable to conscription into the imperial army. The Volga Germans lost their exemption from military service in 1874. The overall structure of the Russian army also contributed to this process: conscripts were dispersed among military units so that national groupings could not develop. The army aimed for no more than 25 per cent of any unit to come from non-Russian groups. As the work of the army was conducted in Russian, conscripts had to become proficient in the language and left the army with a firm command of it.

These pressures on national minorities were designed to Russify their populations and thus to ensure that it was easier for the St Petersburg authorities to control them. Imposing a single language and, by implication, a single culture across the empire was intended to promote this aim. This process was fiercely resisted by many of the national groups which were affected by it. The Baltic German nobility took very limited action by petitioning Alexander III to relax the pro-Orthodox stance which the government was taking. Other national groups in the Baltic provinces countered the imperial government by taking positive action to protect their own national identity. The number of new titles of books published

119

in Latvian rose from 181 printed in 168 000 copies in 1884 to 882 titles in more than five million copies 20 years later. In Poland steps were taken to preserve Polish education by the founding of a Flying University in 1882–3, so-called because it met in different locations each week to avoid the Tsarist authorities. During the two decades of its clandestine existence, this organization grew to a substantial size and provided courses which were equal in content and quality to those provided in official institutions. The variety of actions open to the Finns was more complex than what was available to other national groups. The legislative and legal structures which Finland possessed meant that legislation which affected Finland was dealt with through a specific official, the Minister State-Secretary, who presented matters relating to Finland directly to the Tsar without other St Petersburg ministries necessarily becoming involved. The measures which General Bobrikov devised during his term as Governor-General of Finland between 1898 and 1904 met with substantial resistance from the Finnish Senate which attempted to derail Bobrikov's proposals at every opportunity. It was only in 1910 that Stolypin's government succeeded in legislating to ensure that the St Petersburg government could gain full control of the Finnish government mechanism.

The conservative Russification policies which were the hallmark of the Russian government from 1880 until 1905 failed to achieve their ends and, in some ways, actually intensified national feeling among the non-Russians of the empire. National groups were able to take advantage of the greater freedom of expression in 1905 and after to press their case and to demonstrate that two decades of Russification had done little to quell their aspirations. The Third Congress of the Union for Jewish Equality, meeting in February 1906, declared that Russian Jews must take part in elections to the First Duma 'to stand up for their civil and national interests'.[17] Polish groups too stood on a nationalist platform at the elections. Parallel to the processes taking place elsewhere in Europe, the attempts which the Russian state made to impose a uniform nationality upon its subjects served largely to stimulate national feeling, rather than weaken it. The existence of parliamentary institutions after 1905 provided national groups with a forum in which they could voice their aspirations so that the national clamour inside the Russian Empire was strengthening rather than weakening.

The Russian Empire's national tensions had implications for the state's foreign relations. The steps which the imperial government took to quell the Polish rebellion in 1863 provoked sympathy for the Poles, especially in France, so that any prospect of better relations between Russia and Napoleon III disappeared. The harsh treatment of Russia's Jewish population provoked considerable discontent amongst the international Jewish community which was able to exert pressure on governments to maintain a certain distance in their relations with Russia. This had a particular impact on Russia's need for foreign investment: the Rothschild banking family refused to participate in the financing of a huge loan to Russia in 1906 unless conditions for Jews were improved.[18] Such internal problems proved to be a continuing and unpredictable feature of the way in which Russia was able to conduct its foreign policy.

Between 1855 and 1917 Russian foreign policy was ultimately unsuccessful. During these 60 years Russia was involved in four substantial wars. The Crimean War came to an end in 1856 with the Treaty of Paris, which represented a decisive defeat for Russia. Military success for Russia in the Balkans against the Ottoman Empire in 1877 turned into diplomatic humiliation at the Congress of Berlin the following year, when the other European powers acted to curb Russian influence. War with Japan in 1904–5 produced a comprehensive defeat for Russia both on land and at sea. Russia's involvement in the First World War produced military disappointments, as well as having catastrophic results for the country's internal stability and cohesion. Only one of these four wars provided any degree of military success for Russia – and even that was rapidly negated by diplomacy –

so that Russia proved consistently unable to achieve its foreign policy goals.

Russia's interests outside its own borders were guided by certain long-standing concerns. As the majority of Russia's coastline was ice-bound, Russia had a consistent desire to extend and consolidate its access to ports which would enable it to trade and communicate with the rest of the world all year round. The access to the Baltic Sea which had originally been won by Peter the Great and then extended along both its northern and southern shores allowed St Petersburg and Riga to develop as great ports and industrial centres. The exit from the Baltic, however, was restricted and offered the possibility that it could be closed by powers hostile to Russia. Even though the empire's Black Sea coastline was many hundreds of miles long, Russian access to the Black Sea had even greater limits. The only way out into the Mediterranean was through the Straits which were controlled by the Ottoman Empire. The Russian advance towards the Pacific coast was one way of alleviating the difficulty of access to the open sea, and the Russian state's attitude towards the Ottoman Empire and the Balkans was also very much a product of its desire to obtain greater control over the Black Sea exit. Nikolai Ignatev, Russian ambassador to the Ottoman Empire from 1864 to 1877 wrote that

Russia must become the master in Constantinople . . . either by a Russian becoming governor of the city and the Straits or by seizing the area. There is no other way to ensure permanent protection of Russian interests.[19]

Russian policy-makers also had to take into account nationalist pressures for Russia to play the role of protector towards other Slav nations. This Panslavist approach has particular results for Russia's relations with the Austro-Hungarian and Ottoman empires, since they ruled over Slav peoples such as the Bulgarians, Czechs and Serbs. For Panslavists, these foreign states were oppressing Slav peoples who should be free to govern themselves. They believed that the obvious weakness of the Ottomans during the nineteenth century, together with the exceptional national diversity of Austria-Hungary, meant that the moment had arrived when the Slav peoples could achieve their independence. Ivan Aksakov, a prominent Panslav wrote that

> God has assigned a lofty task to the Russians: to serve the liberation and rebirth of their enslaved and oppressed brethren. There is in Russia no desire for usurpation, no thought of political domination. It desires but the freedom of spirit and life for those Slav peoples which have remained faithful to the Slav confraternity.[20]

In 1858 a Slavonic Committee was established in Moscow and was followed by others in St Petersburg, Kiev and Odessa and, although their membership never rose above 2000, the Panslavist ideas they espoused were effectively disseminated through Katkov's journals and the writings of Professor M. P. Pogodin. This helped to bring about considerable public interest in Russia in the fate of the Balkan Slavs, reflected in Leo Tolstoi's treatment of the topic in *Anna Karenina* and in paintings by members of the *Itinerants* group. This powerful popular sentiment had its impact on elites in Russia; some senior military officers espoused this conservative nationalism,[21] as did bureaucrats. Konstantin Pobedonostsev, who was one of the chief advisers to Alexander III, pressed the Tsar to look favourably on these views, as much for the internal political value which would be gained, as for the lessons which they taught for foreign policy.[22]

While Russia's rulers had pressing political interests which pushed them towards an expansionist foreign policy, there were also important restraints on the state's ability to act abroad. The counter to Russia's desire to acquire more territory and greater access to maritime outlets was that the state was vulnerable and weak in some important respects. Imperial expansion required the military might to secure and defend new territories and yet the condition of Russia's armies was far from satisfactory. By the end of the Crimean War the Russian army was the single largest call on the state's budget, absorbing more than one-third of the state's expenditure, and yet the army's performance in the Crimea had been poor. Despite fighting on their own territory, the Russians proved unable to hold on to the key fortress of Sevastopol, as well as suffering defeats in direct engagements with the British, French and Turkish forces ranged against them. The programme of reform which Alexander II embarked upon in the 1860s included direct action to improve the army. This included changes to the way in which the army was run by establishing a General Staff in 1865 and by dividing the empire into 15 military districts, with the commander of each district enjoying substantial autonomy to ensure that decisions could be taken quickly and effectively. The most wide-ranging change was the introduction of universal conscription in 1874. This meant that instead of the Russian army's soldiers coming exclusively from the peasantry, every young man would now be liable for military service irrespective of his social background. This move was linked to a reduction in the term of military service to six years of active service and nine years in the reserves,[23] which would provide Russia with a much more effective army in times of war.

These changes to the army had some effect on Russia's military capabilities, but the army was still hampered by the difficulty of coping with the very rapid changes that were taking place in military technology. It took over 20 years for the army to be re-equipped, with new rifles and artillery after the Crimean War. But technology was developing so quickly that weapons were superseded before the entire army was equipped, with the result that by the onset of the Russo-Turkish war there was no standard rifle in use throughout the army.[24] These technological changes also caused the army problems in adapting its tactics to fit the new circumstances of warfare: Russian commanders during the Russo-Turkish war continued to send close-packed infantry formations into battle, despite the carnage that followed. The persistent military weakness that afflicted Russia was in evidence again during the Russo-Japanese War when the transport systems of the empire proved inadequate to sustain a conflict at the Far Eastern extremity of the empire. Overall, the Russian military was trying to match the more advanced armies of other states but was attempting to build this on an economic base that did not have the resources to support adequately the rapid modernization of Russia's huge military machine and the attendant infrastructure that this required.

The weakness of the army severely restricted Russia's ability to pursue its foreign interests effectively. This was partly a reflection of Russia's economic backwardness which meant that the pressures placed on the state's budget prevented military expenditure from growing quickly. For ten years after 1884 the military budget was effectively frozen, but the process of modernization also had a less direct impact on Russia's foreign policy. Successive Russian finance ministers, and especially Sergei Witte, believed that Russian industrialization could only be achieved by attracting foreign capital to finance growth. The need to convince foreign investors to put money into Russian industry also demanded that Russia remain on good terms with foreign governments since business and diplomacy were closely linked. This continuing need to attract foreign capital meant that Russia could not afford to alienate other Great Powers, for diplomatic frostiness could easily result in finance drying up and Russia slipping yet further behind the other European states. These practical areas of domestic policy acted as an important restraining influence on Russia's performance on the international stage.

The Crimean War was fought by Russia in the clear expectation that its troops would emerge triumphant. The success of Russian arms in defeating Napoleon, and Alexander I's entry into Paris in the spring of 1814 were still firmly in the minds of the Russian political and military elite, and the reign of Tsar Nicholas I had seen Russia's international standing remain undiminished by military defeat or serious diplomatic reverses. The interest displayed by the French in the Ottoman Empire in the early 1850s therefore provoked Russia to take significant action to protect its own position. The new Emperor Napoleon III of France believed that he could buttress his position at home by demonstrating his concern for the Catholic subjects of the Ottoman Empire. This irritated Russia, since it saw itself as the defender of the Orthodox Christians ruled over by Turkey. Russia believed that any interference by other powers was a threat to its own interests in the region and presaged greater involvement by other European states in the affairs of Turkey with consequences for the overall European balance of power.

When France pressed its case with the Turks for Catholic control of the Holy Places in Jerusalem in 1852, Tsar Nicholas I began to take steps to assert Russia's authority. He sought British support in ensuring that Turkey remained independent and sent Prince A. S. Menshikov, a close adviser, to Constantinople to state Russia's case against the French proposals as well as to claim a Russian protectorate over the Orthodox Christians inside the Ottoman empire. Russia's calculations were based on the belief that Austria would support it and that Britain was not hostile, so felt confident in insisting on a formal treaty to confirm the desired protectorate. Turkey's rejection of this demand provoked Russia to send troops to occupy the territories of Moldavia and Wallachia in 1853. Britain and France, afraid of Russia upsetting the balance of power by gaining too much influence in Turkey and the eastern Mediterranean, declared war on Russia in 1854. The British and French expedition to the Crimea, aimed at the Russian naval base of Sevastopol, proved capable of defeating the Russians on their home territory. The accession of Alexander II in February 1855 prolonged the war: the new Tsar was reluctant to begin his reign by capitulating to foreign powers and it was only in January

1856 that financial pressure and the threat of internal discontent convinced Alexander and his ministers that they had to initiate peace negotiations.

The Treaty of Paris which was concluded in March 1856 imposed awkward terms on Russia. Neither Russia nor Turkey were to be allowed to maintain a navy in the Black Sea, a limitation which bore very heavily indeed on Russia. It limited Russia's European navy to its bases in the Baltic and was a clear slap in the face for Russia's ambitions to extend its influence in the Balkans. The Danube principalities were given their independence and this provided an important impetus towards the creation of an independent Romania, free from domination by Russia. In the following 15 years Russia and its foreign minister, Prince Gorchakov, worked to achieve the annulment of the treaty. Relations with France improved steadily immediately after the end of the war, based on hostility towards Austria from both Russia and France. Austria gave the Russians cause for concern because its Balkan interests could well conflict with Russia's own aspirations, while the French wanted to see Austria's position in Italy restrained. This provided a good base for a degree of *rapprochement* between Russia and France. In 1863, however, relations between the two states sharply deteriorated as a result of Russia's harsh treatment of the Poles. Russia was again isolated.

Russia's international position was very difficult in the wake of this renewed break with France. Assailed again by liberals in Europe over the suppression of the Polish uprising, and still financially and militarily weak in the aftermath of the Crimea, Russia had to bide its time. It was only after the reform programme of the 1860s had helped to restore some of Russia's self-esteem and the state's financial situation had returned to some sort of equilibrium that Russia could undertake a more adventurous foreign role. In addition, the European situation changed dramatically during the late 1860s as Bismarck's Prussia asserted its military and political might with decisive victories over both Denmark and Austria. This evidence of Austrian weakness was important in Russia's October 1870 move to unilaterally renounce the clauses of the Treaty of Paris which limited its naval activity in the Black Sea. The circular in which Gorchakov announced the decision declared that

> The Tsar has in view solely the security and dignity of his empire. He has no intention of reopening the Eastern Question. . . He desires only to preserve and strengthen peace.[25]

This was a somewhat disingenuous statement, as the reassertion of Russian power in the Black Sea region clearly signalled that Russia had no intention of abandoning its interests there. This situation was not displeasing to the newly united German state which saw Austrian weakness as helpful in furthering its attempts to establish its clear domination over the German-speaking peoples of Europe. An 1871 conference in London confirmed Russia's action, allowing it to again maintain a navy on the Black Sea. After his success in the Franco-Prussian war, Bismarck saw clear advantages in establishing a loose alliance of the three great conservative monarchies of Europe and in 1873 this produced the League of Three Emperors between Germany, Austria and Russia. From Russia's point of view, this was a useful step as Russia was becoming increasingly concerned about British intentions in Central Asia and was happy to have some form of support from other European powers in case the balance of advantage in Asia swung too far in Britain's direction.

This alliance also served briefly to moderate St Petersburg's activity in the Balkans. Although the foreign ministry for a time took a more relaxed attitude, this approach was not shared by all those involved in Russian diplomacy and especially by Nikolai Ignatev, the Russian ambassador in Constantinople. Ignatev's firm Panslav views guided the 'forward' policy which he advocated and promoted, sometimes at odds with his masters in St Petersburg. He wanted to enhance

Russian influence by any means possible and gave less thought to the long-term implications that this course of action might have for the stability of the Balkans. By supporting the separatist demands of the Bulgarians, Ignatev helped to foster intense national rivalry in the Balkans.[26] This was to be demonstrated after 1875 when Christians in Herzegovina rebelled and set off a train of events which was to lead to war between Russia and Turkey two years later. This uprising could not be ignored by Serbia or Montenegro, both of which had designs on the Turkish lands, and their aspirations to assert their strength in defence of the Turkish-ruled Balkan Slavs had a striking impact on Russian opinion. Serbia declared war on Turkey in June 1876 and this generated huge pressure amongst Russians for Russia to support its Slav brethren in their fight against the Turks. The weakness of Serbian arms and the outbreak of another Balkan rebellion against the Ottomans in Bulgaria encouraged this attitude and, although Russia made attempts to solve the problem by diplomatic means at the Constantinople conference at the end of 1876, St Petersburg prepared for war.

Austrian neutrality in any war was ensured by an agreement with Russia which effectively determined spheres of influence for the two states in the Balkans. Austria was to hold sway in the west of the region as Russia conceded influence in Bosnia-Herzegovina, while Russian dominance in the eastern Balkans, and especially Bulgaria, was to be confirmed. With this safeguard in place, Russia felt confident in pressing its claims by military means and declared war on Turkey in April 1877. Although the Russians were successful militarily, their agreement with Austria prevented them advancing as far as Constantinople and Russia sought to extract as much as it could from the peace treaty signed with Turkey at San Stefano in March 1878. The main feature of the treaty was the establishment of a large autonomous Bulgarian state, under Russian tutelage. This alarmed other European powers who saw San Stefano as representing a huge increase in Russian influence. Austria-Hungary and Britain were determined to curb Russian expansionism and at the Congress of Berlin in July 1878 they severely reduced the extent of Russia's gains. The Bulgarian state was trimmed in size, Bosnia-Herzegovina were placed under Austrian administration and Serbia, Romania and Montenegro were formally recognized as independent. The diplomatic reverse which Russia suffered in Berlin produced great resentment at home: Panslavs saw the Russian government's acceptance of the congress's outcome as a betrayal of the Balkan Slavs and both government and public harboured a resentment against the European states which had forced this humiliation on Russia.

This failure of Russia's foreign policy in the Balkans left the state again in difficulties. Russia had seen that no other European power was prepared to support her: Austria wanted to protect its own interests in south-eastern Europe, while Germany tried to act as the 'honest broker' in the Balkans rather than supporting the Russian point of view. As the united German state had demonstrated itself to be one of the great European powers, this ambivalence on Bismarck's part gave Russia cause for concern. The Russian government, therefore, had to try to secure its position by building durable alliances. The League of Three Emperors had fallen by the wayside, but Bismarck was convinced that maintaining the balance of power in Europe demanded that this conservative grouping be resurrected.[27] In 1879 Germany and Austria made a defensive agreement in case of Russian attack: the failure of Russia's ambition in the Balkans made Panslavism rather less attractive to the Russian elite and the Russian ambassador in Berlin formally proposed that the League of Three Emperors be revived early in 1880. These Russian overtures met with considerable resistance from Austria, but in mid-1881 agreement was reached. Each of the three states committed itself to neutrality if one of the others was involved in a war with another power. It was also agreed that access to the Black Sea should be closed – which assuaged Russian fears of a British naval attack – and that Austria had the right to annex Bosnia and Herzegovina. This helped to give

Russia some security and the treaty was renewed in 1884 for a further three years.

Russian doubts about the agreement's value, however, came strongly to the fore in 1885 when Bulgaria attempted to assert its independence from Russia. The renewed upsurge of trouble that this brought to the Balkans demonstrated the fragility of the tripartite agreement between Russia, Austria and Germany. It was clear that Austria's interests in the region remained at odds with Russian ambition and that Germany could not bring about any compromise between the other two states. Russia made it plain at the end of 1886 that it was not prepared to renew the League of Three Emperors in its current form when it expired the following year.

Russia needed to turn to other potential sources of diplomatic support. There was little choice available. Russia's rivalry with Britain in Asia meant that there was no immediate opportunity of accommodation in that quarter and that therefore the only potential ally was France. From the French point of view, Russia was an attractive ally: France remained diplomatically isolated after defeat in the Franco-Prussian war and was deeply mistrustful of German ambitions and power. Russia's situation on Germany's eastern frontier meant that a Franco-Russian alliance would exert some restraining influence on Germany. On both sides, therefore, the notion of France and Russia drawing closer together offered a greater degree of security and an escape from diplomatic isolation. In addition it provided some counterweight to British ambition. Early in 1887 France and Russia took joint action to try to counter British influence in Egypt and this was seen as providing some hope for future cooperation.

There was also an important economic element to the Franco-Russian relationship: in 1887 Bismarck ordered the German State Bank to stop accepting Russian securities as collateral for loans. This action had been taken despite the conclusion of the Reinsurance Treaty by Germany and Russia earlier in the year, an agreement significant less for its detailed terms than for its demonstration of Germany's desire to maintain some form of alliance with Russia. The economic dispute between the two states had been sparked off by substantial increases in Russian import duties, designed to promote domestic industrial development, which had a serious impact on Germany, Russia's largest trading partner.[28] The German limitation on extending loans to Russia did not, however, persuade Russia to change its tariff policy, since French banks were keen to take up where the Germans had left off. There were four substantial French loans to Russia between 1888 and 1890 and links between the two states began to develop in other ways. When the deeply conservative Alexander III stood to attention while the French national anthem, the revolutionary hymn the Marseillaise, was played during a visit by a French naval detachment to Russia in 1891, it was clear that official attitudes were changing. Military discussions between the two states took place from 1891 onwards: initially France and Russia simply agreed to consult each other if war was threatened; this developed into a preliminary military convention that was discussed in 1892 and into a full alliance signed in 1894. The Franco-Russian alliance was designed as a clear counter-balance to the Triple Alliance between Germany, Austria and Italy. Russia committed itself to using all its available forces against Germany if France was attacked by Germany or by Italy with German help. France would take similar action should Germany launch an attack on Russia or support Austria in such an attack. France and Russia would both mobilize their armies in response to mobilization by any of the members of the Triple Alliance. The agreement laid down the size of the forces that France and Russia would commit to any war: 1.3 million French troops and between 700 000 and 800 000 Russians would be put into the field against an enemy.

The conclusion of the Franco-Russian alliance had important results. Internationally, it was crucial in formalizing the divisions between European states and, in particular, it meant that Russia's relationship with Germany had undergone a fundamental change. Even though Russia and Germany concluded a commercial agreement later in 1894, it was now clear that Russia regarded the most serious threat to its position as likely to come from the states of the Triple Alliance. The alliance gave considerable impetus to French investment in Russia. It coincided with a period when French domestic government bonds were offering low rates of return and when the economic policies of the Russian government were stimulating economic growth. Although there were periods when French financiers showed less interest in Russia, by 1914 more than 12 000 million francs had been invested in Russia.

The industrial growth Russia experienced during the 1890s was important in turning the state's attention towards the Far East. Finance was available to begin the construction of the Trans-Siberian railway in 1891, and Russian expansion on the Pacific coast continued through the 1890s. This generated constant friction between Russia and Japan. The Japanese were extremely suspicious of Russian ambitions both in China and especially in Korea, seeing this as a direct threat to their own access to mainland China. The Russian presence in Manchuria was strengthened after the Boxer Rising of 1900 when it had sent troops as part of an international effort to restore calm in China, and this encouraged the Russians to seek economic concessions from China. The Chinese eventually persuaded Russia to agree to the removal of its troops by October 1903, but were not prepared to accede to Russia's economic demands. In this situation, Japan looked elsewhere to gain some guarantee of its position and in 1902 concluded an agreement with Britain. This in particular recognized Japan's special position in Korea and provided the Japanese with greater confidence in their dealings with Russia.

In St Petersburg the Russian government was confused over its Far Eastern policy. Sergei Witte, the Minister of Finance, was keen to see Russia's influence expanded by peaceful means and he was supported in this by the Ministers of War and of Foreign Affairs. There were other influences at work, however, with the creation of a vice-royalty for the Far Eastern region and the establishment of a Far Eastern committee in the capital, both of which contributed to calls for a more active policy in the region. This lack of coordination in Russian policy served to make negotiations with Japan difficult and there was little willingness on either side to reach agreement over the Russian position in Manchuria or Japan's influence in Korea. By the beginning of 1904 the Japanese felt confident enough to take military action to secure their demands and in February launched an attack on the Russian base at Port Arthur.

Russia anticipated an easy victory over Japan and it was taken aback by the progress of the war. Japanese forces proved superior to both the Russian army and navy: Port Arthur was besieged and fell at the end of 1904 and the Russian Far Eastern fleet was bottled up in its bases. To strengthen the Russian forces, the Baltic fleet was despatched on an epic journey to the Far East but this resulted in disaster. The Japanese destroyed the fleet at the battle of Tsushima in May 1905 and this, coming on top of a defeat on land at Mukden two months earlier, persuaded the Russian government that it must seek peace. The Treaty of Portsmouth, concluded in August 1905, recognized Japanese superiority in Korea and gave the Liaotung peninsula and the southern part of the island of Sakhalin to Japan. Russia lost the war because its military structures and equipment still needed modernization. Significantly, it was unable to supply and maintain its forces thousands of miles away on the far periphery of the empire when the Trans-Siberian railway was barely complete and only capable of coping with quite small amounts of traffic.

This defeat again compelled Russia to examine its foreign and military policies. The changes to Russian government after 1905 and the establishment of a Council of Ministers which could take an overall view of policy had an impact on Russia's foreign relations. Foreign policy became a subject of debate for the government as a whole, rather than just the preserve of the Tsar and his foreign minister. In Russia after 1905 domestic difficulties made it important to minimize the risk of further foreign entanglements: Stolypin noted that 'our internal situation does not permit us to conduct an aggressive foreign policy'.[29] This had a substantial restraining impact on attempts to pursue an adventurous foreign policy.[30] Russia, therefore, again needed to gain greater security and to ensure that it would not be involved in further conflicts which, as the Far Eastern débâcle had demonstrated, it was ill-equipped to fight. France had concluded an agreement with Britain in 1904 and Russia felt some pressure to improve its relations with France's new ally. Discussions had been taking place between Russia and Britain over their disagreements in Central Asia since 1904 and now Russia accepted a British invitation to resume these talks in 1906.

The result was the Anglo-Russian agreement of 1907 which dealt with these Asian points of friction. Russia agreed to give up its interest in Afghanistan and both powers delimited their respective spheres of influence in Persia, with a neutral zone separating them. Tibet was accepted as neutral by both sides. Although the Russian government saw this agreement with Britain as having exclusively Asian importance, the real significance of this agreement lay in its wider international context. Britain, France and Russia were now linked by treaties and appeared as a counterweight to the Triple Alliance which dominated central Europe. Russia tried hard to prevent Germany and Austria interpreting its alliances as a potential threat. An agreement was made with Germany in 1907 regulating the situation in the Baltic and the following year Alexander Izvolskii, the Russian Foreign Minister, met his Austrian counterpart, Aehrenthal to discuss the situation in the Balkans.

At this meeting, Izvolskii agreed that Russia would accept the full Austrian annexation of Bosnia and Herzegovina as long as Russia received compensation. This enabled him to raise Russia's long-held desire of achieving greater influence in the region and he gained Aehrenthal's agreement to assist in reopening the question of the Straits and allowing access for Russian warships which had been closed by the Congress of Berlin 30 years earlier. When Izvolskii reported back to St Petersburg on the outcome of his meeting at Buchlau, it very quickly became clear that the Russian government as a whole was not prepared to support the foreign minister. Other ministers believed that Russia's apparent abandonment of Slav lands to Austria would create enormous resentment among public opinion and could bring about pressure for military action against Austria. Russia's domestic situation made such a war extremely undesirable since it was perceived that war could upset the fragile balance of domestic peace that had been achieved. While the Austrians proceeded with the annexation and demanded its recognition by Russia, failing which Austria would invade Serbia, Russia could do nothing but accept Austria's demands. The Bosnian crisis of 1908–9 helped to demonstrate the power of the alliance systems in Europe: Germany gave very strong support to Austria in pursuing its Balkan ambitions.

After 1909 the Balkans were again firmly at the forefront of Russian policy. The continuing weakness of the Ottoman Empire and the growing national aspirations of the Balkan peoples persuaded both Austria and Russia to maintain their very close interest in the region. In contrast to the situation in the last part of the nineteenth century, the two powers were now part of formal alliance systems and thus rivalry between them could have implications for European security as a whole. Russia became increasingly prepared to build up resistance in the Balkans to Austrian ambition, rather than taking action itself to limit Austrian influence. In 1912 Russia promoted an alliance between Serbia and Bulgaria which was joined later in the year by Greece to form the Balkan League. The St Petersburg government was warned by its representative in Bulgaria that such an alliance could very easily be used for aggressive purposes and, as predicted, the Balkans were riven by war in 1912 and 1913. The Serbs particularly profited from these two Balkan wars: this alarmed the Austrians who saw an increased threat to their position and moved troops close to their border with Serbia early in 1913. For Russia, the tension between Austria and Serbia was dangerous.

In the years before 1914 Russia was also alarmed by the interest being shown by Germany in the Near East. St Petersburg's representatives in the Ottoman Empire reported growing evidence of German economic and cultural influence in the region.[31] The appointment of a German general, Liman von Sanders, to command the Constantinople garrison late in 1913 was greeted with great concern by the Russian government as it appeared that Germany was making a direct challenge to Russia's desire to control the Straits. When Archduke Franz Ferdinand, the heir to the Austro-Hungarian throne, was assassinated in Sarajevo in June 1914 by a Bosnian Serb nationalist, followed three weeks later by an Austrian ultimatum to Serbia, the Russian government was quick to recognize the part played by German ambition. Sergei Sazonov, the Russian Foreign Minister, was convinced that the delivery of the ultimatum had been timed by Austria and Germany to arrive just after the French President had concluded an official visit to Russia, thus preventing consultation between the two allies on its content.[32] When the Russian Council of Ministers met the day after the ultimatum was issued, it took the view that the situation could be resolved peacefully but that Russia was prepared to go to war to protect Serbia's independence. The government began to make preparations for war, resolving that 'Russia should be ready to make the sacrifices required of her' and deciding in principle to partially mobilize her armies.[33] On 15/28 July Austria declared war on Serbia, thus making war with Russia inevitable. The following day the German ambassador in St Petersburg informed the Russian government that Germany would go to war with Russia if Russia's military preparations did not cease. Russia was by now wholly committed to the Serb cause and could not back down: on

30 July general mobilization was announced and two days later Germany and Russia were at war.

Russia's imperial ambitions were intimately bound up with its relations with foreign states. Its eastward expansion lead ultimately to war with Japan, while Russian designs on Central Asia meant that relations with Britain were strained for half a century. Russian desire to restrain Polish nationalism helped create some community of interest with Austria, and especially with Germany, as both states had annexed other areas of Poland when the state was partitioned at the end of the eighteenth century. The crux of Russia's imperial and foreign activities, however, was the Balkans. Russian Panslavism combined with the nascent nationalism of the peoples of south-eastern Europe to galvanize Russian public opinion in favour of Slav solidarity, and against both Turkish and Austrian influence in the region. At the same time, Russia's long-held desire to take advantage of the decline of the Ottoman empire allowed the government to try persistently to gain control of the Straits, and thus allow its fleet free passage from the Black Sea into the Mediterranean. National and international concerns thus fused to make a potent mix. Russian involvement in the First World War came as a direct result of its Balkan ambitions and was to prove fatal to the Tsarist regime.

5

The End of the Old Order

When Nicholas II appeared on the balcony of the Winter Palace in St Petersburg the day after war was declared in the summer of 1914, the huge crowd which had gathered in the square below greeted him rapturously. Some Russians saw this as indicative of a new mood in the country. Late in 1914, a Moscow landowner wrote that

> With the atmosphere which I have seen to exist in the army, and with the mood of the people which is heard of on all sides, we cannot fail to be victorious ... I already see the forerunners of the future ... soberness, and general love and goodwill.[1]

Not everyone in Russia, however, had such optimism and enthusiasm about the war. In February 1914 Peter Durnovo, the 70-year-old former Minister of Internal Affairs and leader of the conservative group in the State Council, wrote a memorandum in which he argued that a war with Germany would be disastrous for Russia. He dreaded the economic outcome of a war, arguing that Russia did not have the financial resources to engage in a major European conflict and that either victory or defeat would bring deeply un-favourable economic consequences. With what proved to be uncanny foresight, Durnovo predicted that 'there must inevitably break out in the defeated country a social revolution which, by the very nature of things, will spread to the country of the victor'.[2]

The Russian armies had mixed fortunes in the opening months of the First World War. Immediately war was declared, the Russians began to advance westwards into East Prussia. This rapid move was dictated by the nature of Russia's alliance with France: German war plans envisaged concentrating its forces in the west to achieve a quick and decisive victory against France. This assumed that Russia would be slow to mobilize its troops and that, once victory over France was assured, Germany could then move troops eastwards before the Russian armies were ready to stage offensive action. The Russian advance into East Prussia in August 1914 helped to put paid to these pre-war calculations of the military planners by compelling the Germans to devote substantial forces to the eastern front. As with every other combatant army during the first months of the war, the Russians proved unprepared for the nature of the conflict that took place. Cavalry proved useless against the withering fire that artillery and rifles could deliver. These new weapons were able to consume ammunition at a rate far beyond what strategists had imagined. The number of casualties was huge. In the battles of Tannenberg and the Masurian Lakes in August and September 1914, both Russia and Germany lost large numbers of men: 100 000 Germans were killed or taken prisoner and more than 170 000 Russians. The defeat which Russia suffered in East Prussia resulted in the loss of territory to Germany and gave a severe blow to morale. This, however, was partly compensated for by success further south against the Austro-Hungarian forces. Russia invaded Galicia and was able to inflict defeats on Austria, capturing the provincial capital of Lvov early in September 1914.

The first winter of the war was one of stalemate. Russia's

communications with its allies was hampered by the entry of Turkey into the war alongside Germany and Austria, since this meant that the Russian Black Sea ports were rendered useless, not just for naval traffic but also for normal commerce. In the spring of 1915 the Germans and Austrians launched offensives against Russia and achieved significant success. Between May and September 1915 Russia lost all the Austrian territory in Galicia which it had gained the previous year, while the Germans too pushed eastwards. Warsaw fell to the Germans in August and Russia lost control of all its industrially important Polish provinces. By the autumn, German troops were close to the great industrial city of Riga on the southern shore of the Baltic. The retreat of 1915 was disastrous for Russia in terms of the territory and resources that it lost, but the losses of manpower were at least as significant. More than a million Russian soldiers were killed during the year and a further million taken prisoner.[3] One direct result of Russian military weakness during 1915 was a change in the supreme command of the army. The Tsar's uncle, Grand Duke Nikolai Nikolaevich, had been appointed as Commander-in-Chief on the outbreak of war but in August 1915, Nicholas II decided to take over the job himself. Although the Tsar was warned by his ministers that this move would automatically mean that he would be seen as responsible for any reverses which the army suffered, Nicholas went ahead and assumed command.

Russian military fortunes improved in the 1916 campaigning season. General Brusilov commanded an offensive against Austria which enabled the Russian armies to repeat some of the gains they had originally made two years earlier in Galicia. There was failure, however, when Russian armies in the north attempted to match this success by attacking German forces. After three seasons of war, Russia's military position appeared to be improving a little. In some ways the Russian armed forces had performed more effectively than had been expected, having begun the war without completing a programme of modernization begun after 1908.

141

In 1914 sections of the Russian officer corps had been deeply concerned over the inadequacy of preparation for war and over shortages of equipment. It was reported that the Navy Minister himself had grave doubts about the ability of Russia's Baltic fleet to take on the German navy.[4] The fighting had, however, taken a huge toll on the country's armed forces. The enormous size of the Russian armies had proved insufficient to make a decisive breakthrough against either Germany or Austria. Any success was limited or short-lived. Nearly 1.5 million men of the Russian armed forces had been killed, more than four million wounded and over two million had been taken prisoner.

Fighting a European war placed great strains on the Russian economy. Before 1914 Germany had been Russia's largest trading partner. This market for Russian exports disappeared overnight and Russian industry was deprived of imports from Germany. Trade was severely disrupted by the blockade of the Baltic, the closure of the Black Sea and the limitation placed by the Swedish government on trade in arms across its territory. The only feasible outlets for Russian trade were the Arctic ports of Archangel and Murmansk and the Far Eastern ports at the end of the Trans-Siberian railway. These all presented great difficulty of access for Russian business, as each was located at the end of a long and inadequate railway line. The volume of Russia's foreign trade declined sharply. During 1914–15 imports fell by 40 per cent and exports declined by the same proportion over the first two years of the war.

The demands which the military themselves placed upon the economy were severe. Almost 15 million men served in the Tsarist forces during the first three years of war and the dislocation that conscription brought to the labour force was considerable. The balance of the labour force was also upset by the pressures imposed on it by Russia's need to increase its industrial production, partly to compensate for the difficulty of importing goods and partly to supply the enormous armies that Russia put into the field. Although there was a complicated system of exemptions from military service, many industrial workers did not escape being called up. Of the industrial labour force in Petrograd – St Petersburg's name from 1914 – 40 000 were lost to the army between 1914 and 1916.[5] This coincided with industry itself requiring a greatly increased labour force to cope with the demand for higher output. The number of industrial workers in the capital grew by more than 60 per cent between 1914 and 1917 and factories were still hungry for more labour, sometimes resorting to paying higher wages to attract workers. The Russian coal mining industry expanded during the war, partly in response to the near-impossibility of importing coal from Britain. Its labour force doubled to reach 800 000. Faced with transporting millions of soldiers across the empire, and with the need to keep them supplied and equipped, the Russian railway system took on nearly 400 000 more employees during the war.

Russian industry did not find it an easy task to adapt to the demands of wartime. The belief that any European war would be a short one had led Russian military strategists to concentrate on building up stocks of arms and ammunition, believing that they would suffice for the six-month conflict they expected. They had given no thought to ensuring that armaments factories were ready to increase production quickly and maintain supplies over a long period. As a result, when it became clear that the war was going to last much longer than anticipated and that the nature of the fighting dictated the need for huge quantities of weaponry, the Russian armaments industry had great difficulty in coping with the changed circumstances. The Tula rifle factory, the largest in the empire, produced only 16 rifles during the first seven months of 1914.[6] The crisis of armaments supply was at its most severe during 1915: the Russian armed forces estimated that they would need 3.5 million artillery shells each month and yet during the first four months of the year they received a total of only two million shells. The supply of rifles was equally poor. Russian industry was not able to meet the demands placed upon it: it could not obtain the foreign – largely German – machinery needed to expand armaments factories and by the summer of 1915 domestic production of shells was running at only one million per month, less than one-third of the quantity the army needed. Inadequate levels of arms and ammunition made a substantial contribution to Russia's military setbacks of 1915.

After 1915 the performance of Russian industry improved substantially. Factories switched to producing munitions, as demand for these products was guaranteed. Production of basic resources such as coal and oil increased. Equally important, however, were the moves taken to coordinate the industrial war effort. The government involved selected representatives of industry and commerce in planning military supply from May 1915, and significant steps were taken by Russian industrialists themselves. When the congress of the Association of Trade and Industry met in May 1915 the leading Moscow industrialist, P. P. Riabushinskii, declared that 'each factory, each mill, all of us must only think of that which can overcome this enemy force'.[7] The congress decided to encourage the formation of regional war-industries commit-tees and itself created a central committee to include representatives of the regional organizations, from local government and science and technology. Orders to small companies could be channelled through the committees and representatives sat on government bodies dealing with food, fuel and transport. By 1916 the overall output of Russian industry was 20 per cent higher than in 1913. Coal output increased by 30 per cent, and the engineering and chemical industries more than doubled their production. The 5 per cent of production which went to the military before the war had increased to 30 per cent. This shift in the emphasis of Russian industry was accompanied by a sharp reduction in the output of consumer goods. Consumption by households fell by 25 per cent during the war.[8]

The demands of the army and of war industries for labour had a substantial impact on the Russian countryside. It was the villages which supplied most of the conscripts and most of the additional labour for the factories. As the war went on, this had an increasing effect on agricultural communities. Women had to take on a larger share of farm work: by 1916 they made up more than 70 per cent of the agricultural labour force on peasant farms and nearly 60 per cent of workers on landowners' estates. The army requisitioned large numbers of horses so that the number of peasant households without a horse rose from 25 per cent to 30 per cent. Though agricultural work became more difficult, the peasantry did gain some advantages from the war. The departure of millions of peasants from the countryside to the army or the city meant that less food was consumed in the villages themselves. While the army did requisition horses, compensation was paid to the peasants and peasant families also received allowances if their menfolk were conscripted. The regime of prohibition, introduced by the government at the beginning of the war in a fit of patriotic enthusiasm, acted to reduce peasant expenditure by making vodka unavailable.[9] Prices for agricultural produce rose during the war, so that grain prices doubled between 1913 and 1916. Peasants who produced a surplus could therefore increase their notional income.

The additional money that this brought into the villages was, however, of little use to peasant producers as there were insufficient manufactured goods available at reasonable prices for them to buy. The prices of manufactured goods rose, however, at roughly the same rate as agricultural prices and, with Russian industry's move away from the production of consumer goods, there was less available in the shops. Inflation accelerated as the war progressed so that by the end of 1916 prices were three times the level of 1913. In these cir-cumstances, it is not surprising that the peasants saw little in-centive to produce substantial surpluses. The area of land under cultivation shrank during the war. By 1916, 12 per cent less land was being devoted to growing grain and potatoes and the amount harvested decreased by at least as much.

By 1916–17 the quantity of grain harvested was almost 20 per cent less than in 1913.[10] This reduction in the quantity of food being grown was rendered even more serious by the peasants' reluctance to sell their produce. Before the war only about 25 per cent of the total amount of grain harvested had been marketed, and the rest retained by the producers for their own consumption. By 1916–17 the proportion of the harvest which was available had declined by 30 per cent as the peasants ate more themselves, used the grain to distil the spirits they could no longer buy legally or simply stored their grain in the hope of better times to come.

The problem of food supply to the cities and to the army was also exacerbated by the inadequacy of the transport system across the empire. The industrial areas of the empire and the provinces which did not grow enough to feed their own inhabitants were generally located in the north and centre of Russia, with Moscow and Petrograd as their largest centres. Effective transport was needed to move produce from the grain-rich areas to the south and the new needs of the army, which now consumed as much as the cities, now meant that food also had to be moved to the front line along Russia's western frontier. The Russian railway system had to adjust to a wholly different pattern of traffic after 1914: both the number of passengers and the amount of freight grew, but military traffic took precedence over everything else. In any case, railways in the west of the empire came under the direct control of the military authorities. Despite laying more track and buying more locomotives and wagons, the railway system found it difficult to cope. The quantity of grain transported by rail fell by more than 30 per cent between 1913 and 1915. The government tried to take action to improve the food situation. Early in 1915 it allowed local officials to fix prices for agricultural produce and, if this was ineffective, to requisition food at a lower price. This failed to improve the situation and moves to regulate prices nationally for some goods, such as flour and sugar, similarly failed. With rapidly increasing food prices, producers and traders were unwilling to sell at the regulated price because they could obtain a better deal on the free market. In September 1916 grain itself came under the price regulation regime and this served to further reduce incentives on farmers to put their produce on the market. Army rations had to be cut: the amount of bread soldiers received was reduced at the end of 1916. Deliveries of food to the cities declined. The government's food supply organization estimated that Petrograd needed more than 12 000 railway wagons of food each month to feed the population adequately. In the seven months after July 1916, this target was achieved only twice and in January 1917 the capital received only 6556 wagons which included less than 10 per cent of its requirements of rye flour.[11]

The wartime performance of the Russian economy did enable the army to continue fighting. Industry recovered from the initial dislocation which war brought, and by 1916 the levels of production of military equipment encouraged the generals to look to the future with optimism. The First World War was a very different type of war, however, from anything which had preceded it. While the military implications of this were eventually digested, there was less recognition of the extensive impact which the war had on the civilian population. The economy of war brought dramatic adjustments to the patterns of consumption and production in both agriculture and industry. Pressure was exerted on both peasant farmers to produce more food and on industrial workers to increase their output. The composition of the labour force changed: industry's need for more workers meant that untrained men and women were put into factories that were operating flat out. The use of refugees and prisoners of war as agricultural workers often produced tensions in the villages. The economic demands of this first 'total war' placed stresses beyond even those predicted by Durnovo on Russian society.

The war also placed great strain on Russia's political system.

A special session of the Fourth Duma was held a week after the declaration of war at which every party, other than the five Bolsheviks, voted for war credits, the additional finance which the government needed to embark on a war. The Duma chairman, Mikhail Rodzianko, declared in his speech that 'the war has put a sudden end to all our domestic strife . . . the Russian people has not known such a wave of patriotism since 1812'.[12] The government moved quickly to assert its authority in the face of war: censorship was re-introduced and large areas of western Russia were placed under martial law. Although the composition of the Duma was firmly angled towards the centre and right of Russian politics, with more than 40 per cent of the deputies repre-senting parties that were explicitly right-wing, the govern-ment was extremely suspicious of the Duma's intentions. In the year before war broke out V. A. Maklakov, the Minister of Internal Affairs, had twice made proposals to emasculate the Duma by removing its legislative powers and leaving it as a purely consultative body. The special sitting of the Duma in July 1914 lasted only a single day and the government was extremely reluctant to allow the Duma to meet again, permitting a further three-day sitting only at the end of January 1915.

The impotence of political groups to exert any influence through the national forum of the Duma helped to stimulate local initiatives to allow a degree of public participation in the war effort. Representatives of local government institutions established the Unions of Towns and of Zemstvos in the autumn of 1914 with the initial aim of organizing the care of the wounded by providing a network of fully equipped hospitals. By 1917 the Union of Towns employed 54 000 people.[13] In the spring of 1915 the two bodies were allowed to establish a joint organization, known as Zemgor, and its activities ranged considerably wider than the original remit of its two partners. Zemgor took the lead in organizing the evacuation of industrial plant from Riga when the city was threatened with capture by the Germans in the summer of

1915, and it also played a part in the procurement of military equipment from Russian industry. The importance of these organizations, along with the war-industries committees, was not so much in the actual work that they carried out, useful though this was, but in the forum which they provided for the politically and socially conscious Russian middle classes to articulate their views.

Russia's military reverses in the spring of 1915 brought political tensions as well. The wholesale loss of territory to German and Austrian troops made Russian weakness all too evident to Russian society in general and raised critical questions, not just about the competence of the empire's military leadership, but also about the political direction of the country. Politically aware society believed that the failure of Russian arms demonstrated the pressing need for the political process to be opened up to allow them real participation in the work of government. The government itself was split over this issue. Some ministers such as Alexander Krivoshein, the Minister of Agriculture, had considerable sympathy with calls for reform. In response to pressure from like-minded members of the government, the Tsar dismissed some of his most conservative ministers including Sukhomlinov, the Minister of War, and Maklakov, Minister of Internal Affairs, but retained the 75-year-old Ivan Goremykin as Chairman of the Council of Ministers.

Members of the Duma pressed for it to be recalled to discuss the deteriorating military situation. When it did meet in mid-July 1915 the Duma launched vigorous attacks on the government's handling of the war, going so far as to demand Sukhomlinov's arraignment for treason as Minister of War during the first year of the conflict. Although following the initial burst of criticism, the Duma stressed its support for the overall direction of the war and emphasized that it wanted only to root out incompetence, the opinions that were voiced by deputies generated substantial anger among the deeply conservative elements surrounding the Tsar and in the government. The aged Goremykin wanted to see the

Duma's session brought to an end as quickly as possible. The threat of dissolution served only to polarize political opinion still further by uniting the majority of the Duma deputies in direct opposition to the government.

Faced with a government which rejected the idea that the political parties could play any formal part in the war effort, nearly 70 per cent of the deputies in the Duma joined in the formation of the Progressive Bloc. Based on the centrist Octobrist party and on the liberal Kadets, the Bloc also drew support from the Progressive Nationalists on the right and the Progressists on the left. The central demand of the Bloc's August 1915 programme was

> The formation of a unified government of individuals who have the confidence of the country and are in agreement with the legislative institutions about the need for the rapid implementation of a definite programme.[14]

The members of the Progressive Bloc were deeply frustrated with the reluctance of the Tsar and his ministers to involve them fully in the war effort, especially when Russia's performance was so dismal. They advocated a range of specific measures which they believed would provide the internal stability which was necessary to bring the war to a successful conclusion. These included the improvement of the rights of non-Russian nationalities, greater freedom for trade unions, reform of local government and an amnesty for individuals who had been convicted of political or religious offences, as well as a general demand for an end to arbitrary government. Although the Bloc received the tacit support of most government ministers, its programme was viewed by Goremykin and Nicholas II as wholly unacceptable. Parallels with 1905 were clear in the minds of the Tsar and his chief minister: the Progressive Bloc was a further attempt to present the agenda of change which had originally been put forward in 1905 and which the regime had been able to counter as it reasserted its authority as disturbances died down.

The political pressure on the Tsar and his Prime Minister was made more intense by the protests against Nicholas's decision to take over the post of Commander-in-Chief. Eight ministers appealed to the Tsar not to take this step, as did Rodzianko, the Duma chairman. Nicholas II would not, however, budge from his decision. Goremykin, although almost isolated inside the government in his opposition to the demands of the Progressive Bloc, did have one card which he believed would silence the cacophony of criticism of the government which was coming from moderate Russian political opinion. He persuaded Nicholas II to prorogue the Duma at the beginning of September 1915, much to the fury of other ministers. The secretary of the Council of Ministers described the scene at its meeting when Goremykin announced this decision:

> Sazonov [Minister of Foreign Affairs] was particularly upset and virtually hysterical by the end of the meeting . . . Polivanov [Minister of War] was boiling over with bile and looked ready to bite; he behaved quite indecently towards the Chairman. Krivoshein [Minister of Agriculture] looked hopelessly sad and anxious. Ignatev [Minister of Education], as he always does in difficult times, was violently messing up his sparse hair.[15]

The political crisis of 1915 demonstrated the absolute intransigence of the Tsar and his closest advisers. They were wholly unwilling to accept that any other group had a right to participate in the work of government, even when deep crisis faced the Russian state. The members of the Progressive Bloc believed that Russia's dismal performance in the war stemmed from the failure of its political system to draw society together and that the increasing isolation of the Tsar and his ministers from political opinion and from society in general would only exacerbate the situation. The government clearly believed that making any sort of concession to moderate opinion might mark a return to the dangerous days immediately after 1905, when political parties caught the scent of reform in the air and believed that they could use the new constitutional arrangements to bring about radical change. By rejecting conciliation, the monarchy had pushed moderate opinion towards adopting a much more vigorous attitude of opposition.

The Tsar and his chief minister were assured of support from powerful elements in seeking to resist the Progressive Bloc. From the summer of 1915 Nicholas II spent most of his time at military headquarters in Mogilev in western Russia and his wife, the Empress Alexandra, was able to exert considerable influence over Nicholas's perception of political developments in the capital. The Empress had always kept herself aloof from society and her German birth increased her isolation during the war years. The heir to the throne, Alexei, suffered from haemophilia: Grigorii Rasputin, a monk who appeared to be able to stop the child's bleeding, became an increasingly close confidant of the Empress during the war and was also able to influence the advice which Alexandra gave to her husband. The Empress put her preferences for ministerial appointments forcefully in her letters to Nicholas, often supporting her arguments by referring to Rasputin's views. In the summer of 1916 she wrote

> Gregory begs you earnestly to name Protopopov [as Minister of the Interior]. You know him and had such a good impression of him, happens to be of the Duma (is not Left) and so will know how to be with them.[16]

The mentally unstable Protopopov was duly appointed Minister of the Interior in September 1916. Outside the court itself, political parties on the right received direct financial support from the government, while congresses of monarchist organizations voiced their disapproval of the Progressive Bloc.

The regime felt sufficiently confident of its position to postpone a further session of the Duma planned for November 1915, and believed that its brusque treatment of the Progressive Bloc had effectively neutralized this source of opposition. Although Goremykin left his post in January 1916, he was replaced by Boris Sturmer, an equally strong supporter of the policy of keeping moderate political parties on the margins of political life. This was to be only the first in the game of 'ministerial leapfrog' that took place during 1916: there were three holders of the chairmanship of the Council of Ministers through the year, four Ministers of the Interior, three Ministers of Justice and three Ministers of Foreign Affairs. This rapid turnover of men at the top of the Russian government represented an attempt to find some way of coping with the increasingly adverse effects which the war was having on the empire. Simply changing ministers could not, however, solve the difficulties which the war was creating for Russian society as a whole.

These problems also provoked members of political parties to voice their deep discontent with the government more and more stridently. When the Duma met in November 1916 Paul Miliukov, the Kadet party leader, delivered a speech full of anger at the incompetence of the government and of frustration at the inability he and like minded people felt to persuade the government to change its policies. He asked

When the Duma declares again and again that the home front must be organized for a successful war and the government continues to insist that to organize the country means to organize a revolution – is this stupidity or treason?[17]

Even though the government tried to censor reports of the speech in the press, illicit copies quickly reached the provinces and gave wide currency to Miliukov's imprecations against the government. The political situation at the end of 1916 was very difficult. The estrangement between government and moderate political opinion was complete; the desire of the Progressive Bloc parties to participate in the work of government was perceived by the regime as representing

153

an ambition to seize power for themselves. The social elite of the empire was far from being united behind the monarch: in December 1916 Rasputin was murdered by a small group, which included a cousin of the Tsar, in the belief that his removal from the scene would help to save the monarchy. Most ominously for the Tsarist regime, however, the mood of the population across the empire was becoming disturbed and ugly as 1916 wore on.

Popular discontent penetrated most sections of Russian society within the first two years of the war. Even during the initial process of mobilization in 1914, peasant soldiers had not demonstrated any great enthusiasm for the war.[18] The nature of the war that they were forced to fight served to increase their unhappiness. The level of casualties was very high; nearly 400 000 men were killed during the first six months of the war. The problems of military supply during 1915 and the wholesale retreat of the Russian army increased the rate at which men were killed and wounded or taken prisoner. These huge losses during the first year of the war meant that the army was increasingly filled with raw, untrained peasant soldiers who were wholly unprepared for the difficult and unpleasant conditions which they had to endure. Desertion was a problem from 1915 onwards. Soldiers resented the cuts in their rations that resulted from the reduced amount of food coming onto the market. The army was not insulated from the political and economic crises that were developing across the empire. Disquiet about the competence of the government and of the military high command quickly spread through the officer corps and it was difficult to conceal officers' doubts from the ordinary soldiers. When soldiers went home on leave they could see for themselves the increasingly difficult economic situation, and while they were at the front, letters to and from home helped to keep both the soldiers and their families up to date with the conditions in which they both lived. During the autumn of 1916 there were mutinies in a dozen regiments as the stresses of the war took their toll. The Russian army was not alone in experiencing this phenomenon as the conflict dragged on, but the particularly wide-ranging difficulties which beset the Russian Empire during the war made these mutinies especially ominous.

There was also discontent among the peasantry. Farmers' growing reluctance to market food supplies affected country dwellers as much as it did townspeople. Many peasants needed to buy food on the open market to supplement their own produce; high prices and shortages caused problems in the villages. The shift of the economy away from the production of consumer goods meant that, even if the peasantry were prepared to market their food, there was much less available on which to spend the proceeds. As inflation gathered pace during 1916, there was no incentive for the peasant to hold cash and this made farmers even less willing to sell produce. Economic stresses were not the only problems which the Russian countryside experienced. Police reports in October 1916 noted that

> High prices affect the country no less than the towns: in the country as well they bring with them improbable rumours, even more fantastic than those heard in the towns. The peasantry willingly believe rumours about the export of leather, grain, sugar etc to Germany . . . Everything makes the atmosphere of the countryside very troubled.[19]

The extension of martial law to much of western Russia also provided cause for unhappiness among the rural population, as the transfer of authority from the civil power to the military removed many of the safeguards for individual rights that had been achieved after 1905. During the war the number of peasant disturbances rose: in the second half of 1914 there were 265 instances of rural discontent and 13 per cent of these required the use of troops to put them down. There was a respite during the following year, but in 1916 troops had to be used to deal with more than 30 per cent of the 300 or so disturbances.[20]

The cities, however, bore the brunt of the economic crisis. The demand for factory labour grew as Russian industry expanded: women and children made up an ever larger proportion of the labour force while working conditions deteriorated. The number of industrial accidents increased, so that more than 18 per cent of the 22 000 employees at the enormous Putilov engineering works suffered some form of injury at work in the first nine months of 1915.[21] Factories demanded that their employees work longer hours while wages in some industries, especially those which employed a large proportion of women, failed to keep pace with rising prices.[22] Living conditions became more difficult as the great influx of new workers tried to find housing in already overcrowded cities and as food supplies became scarcer. One way in which discontent was expressed was through strikes. Economic conditions made many people stop work, especially those in the textile industry who were suffering from the low wages paid to a largely female labour force. In 1915 when the Germans were advancing rapidly eastwards, strikers in Moscow demanded the removal of managers of German origin and took action against property that they suspected to be German-owned. There were also strikes to protest at the political situation and, especially in Petrograd, they outnumbered strikes motivated by economic reasons. Nearly a million Petrograd workers participated in strikes during the war, two-thirds of them for political reasons. As the war progressed, the number of strikes grew, particularly in the key defence industries and by 1916 an average of more than 80 000 defence workers were on strike each month; a five-fold increase on the previous year.

The economic situation in the cities and particularly in Petrograd deteriorated sharply at the end of 1916. The winter was particularly hard that year and demand for fuel and food intensified. Supplies to the cities, however, were reaching new lows and the price of what little was available rocketed. In Moscow the cost of charcoal increased almost three-fold in the six months after September 1916, while in Petrograd the price of milk went up by 40 per cent during December 1916 and January 1917. It was the availability of bread, however, which gave the greatest concern. Faced with continuing reductions in the delivery of flour to the capital, the authorities decided on 19 February to introduce rationing and restrict bread consumption. This gave a huge impetus to the strike movement which had been growing since the beginning of the year. More than 140 000 Petrograd workers marked the anniversary of Bloody Sunday on 9 January by going on strike and, although there were no mass demonstrations, some regions of the capital were effectively at a standstill for the day. The same process was taking place in Moscow. Strikes spread during January and February as workers demanded higher wages in an attempt to counter the food shortages and, by implication, attacked the government for its inability to ensure adequate supplies in the cities. Revolutionary political parties, including the Bolsheviks, tried to orchestrate the strike movement, but the anger of working people was so powerful that the strikes gathered pace without any need for external encouragement.

On 23 February textile workers in the northern district of Petrograd stopped work and took to the streets, calling for bread and trying to reach the city centre to publicize their grievances. The police were able to restrict the strikers' movements and to largely exclude them from the heart of Petrograd. Within 24 hours the movement had taken on the character of a general strike as nearly 200 000 workers left their jobs, and a further 70 000 joined them the next day. The capital was effectively paralysed by 25 February and the police and the garrison had extreme difficulty in controlling the crowds of demonstrators that filled the streets. On the direct order of the Tsar, troops opened fire on marchers on 26 February, killing more than 50 people, and the government expected that, as in 1905, this would serve to restore order and to put an end to the demonstrations. The regime had not reckoned with the impact of the war on the army and did not understand that its soldiers were suffering from the same privations that had provoked working people to breaking point. On 27 February large sections of the Petrograd garrison mutinied and refused to obey the order to suppress the popular revolt by force.

The Duma had met on 14 February and its leaders tried to take advantage of the disturbances to again press their case for a new government. On 26 February, Rodzianko despatched a telegram to Nicholas II, insisting that 'It is necessary that some person who enjoys the confidence of the country be entrusted at once with the formation of a new government. There must be no delay.'[23] The regime rejected this demand out of hand, believing that firm action would win it the day and, as well as ordering military action to pacify Petrograd, it approved the prorogation of the Duma. On the same day that soldiers in the capital mutinied, members of the Duma decided to form a temporary committee to ensure that their voice could still be heard, but the situation deteriorated so quickly overnight that on 28 February it determined to take power itself to restore order. The existing government put up no resistance as the Winter Palace was occupied by troops supporting the revolution.

Nicholas II was at army headquarters in Mogilev, 600 km south of Petrograd, when the revolution began. Ordering troops to move towards the capital to suppress the revolt, he set off by train to return north. Beginning to appreciate the seriousness of the situation he faced only when his train was prevented from approaching the capital, the Tsar was still reluctant to make any political concessions. The military, however, were deeply worried by the reports they received of the revolution spreading to Moscow and to the key naval base of Kronstadt in the Baltic. Nicholas eventually agreed to the formation of a government responsible to the Duma on 2 March, but events in Petrograd had by then overtaken him. Alongside the establishment of the Duma committee, socialist intellectuals had established – in the same building – the Petrograd Soviet of Workers' Deputies. The pressure from the Soviet was for a republic. In an attempt to preserve the principle of monarchy in Russia, his military commanders and Rodzianko advised him to abdicate. Late on 2 March 1917 he agreed to renounce the throne in favour of his brother, Grand Duke Michael. The following day Michael refused the crown and the Tsarist autocracy had ended.

The February Revolution brought about the collapse of the Romanov dynasty and the replacement of the government by an administration dominated by liberals who had been at the forefront of the demands for reform. The government was headed by Prince G. E. Lvov, while Miliukov took on the foreign affairs portfolio, and Alexander Guchkov, a leading member of the Octobrist party and a Moscow businessman, became Minister of War. This was a Provisional Government, holding the reins until a Constituent Assembly could be elected to determine a new constitution and the permanent form of government for Russia. The Provisional Government proved, however, to be little more stable than its predecessors. In the seven months following the Tsar's abdication, four administrations held power. The political problems of 1917 stemmed from the limited power which the government held. The successive Provisional Governments were well aware that they held no real legitimacy as they were essentially self-appointed and were thus reluctant to take any fundamental decision; such matters were to be the preserve of the Constituent Assembly. At the same time, the Petrograd Soviet was joined by hundreds of Soviets that were formed right across Russia and they could claim to represent the ordinary people of Russia with greater justification than the Provisional Government. The Petrograd Soviet came to act in parallel to the administration, able to veto its decisions but unwilling to actually participate in the government's work.

The key issue which confronted the Provisional Government was the war. Order No. 1 issued by the Petrograd Soviet at the beginning of March had stated that the army should only obey orders from its commanders if they were in accordance with those of the Soviet, and it posed a further challenge to the authority of officers by calling for the ordinary soldiers in each unit to elect a committee which would look after the unit's weapons. The government found itself trying to fight a major war with forces where the division between officers and ordinary soldiers was growing and where the rank and file increasingly questioned the need to continue fighting. While the Russian government continued to declare to its allies that it was determined to continue the struggle and emerge victorious, the evidence of desertions – running at more than 100 000 for March alone – placed a question mark over Russia's ability to live up to these commitments.

The most significant impact of the political revolution was on the ordinary people of Russia. Political authority disintegrated during 1917 not just in the capital but also in provincial towns and cities across the state. The collapse of Tsarism released a vast store of expectations: almost every social group had grievances that it believed would be resolved by a change of government. The peasantry believed that there would be a general redistribution of land and that this would give them access to the land held by large landowners. Between March and October 1917 there were more than 4000 recorded instances of peasant unrest,[24] including more than 900 occurrences each of seizure of estate land and of illegal woodcutting. Working people found that their living conditions continued to deteriorate after the collapse of the monarchy, rather than showing any sign of improvement. Inflation continued apace: prices more than doubled during 1917 and real wages fell by half. Strikes did not cease with the disappearance of the autocracy; in Moscow alone there were 269 work stoppages involving more than 250 000 workers between March and October 1917.[25] In some of the areas populated by non-Russians, the disintegration of central authority provided an opportunity for nationalist activists to intensify their work. The Provisional Government was wholly unable to stem the tide of discontent which swept Russia; it was unable to assert its authority across the state and was unwilling to take any action which could be seen as pre-empting the work of the Constituent Assembly.

February 1917 transformed the latent discontent in Russian society into full-scale social disintegration. Once the coercive apparatus of Tsarism had disappeared, each element of Russian society was able to express its grievances openly and with little fear of retribution. In a situation where central government authority was weak and where the ties that bound provincial administration to the centre had loosened dramatically, it was easy for extreme political groups to gain influence. Lenin had returned to Petrograd from exile in Switzerland at the beginning of April 1917 and had insisted in his 'April Theses' that the Bolsheviks should refuse to support the Provisional Government and should aim at making a socialist revolution. The distance which the Bolsheviks kept from the Provisional Government and from other socialist parties was very helpful to them. Party membership increased enormously during 1917 to reach perhaps 250 000 by the autumn,[26] and Bolshevik influence in the cities grew. The left of Russian politics was strengthened by General Kornilov's vain attempt in August to stage a counter-revolution and Lenin began to argue that the time was approaching when the Bolsheviks would be in a position to stage an insurrection and seize power. In mid-October the Petrograd Soviet, chaired by Trotskii, established a Military Revolutionary Committee, ostensibly to organize the defence of the city against the encroaching Germans. This quickly enabled the Bolsheviks to gain control of the garrison and on 25 October they used this force – and the Red Guards, a workers' militia – to seize control of Petrograd and to disband the Provisional Government. Power passed to the Congress of Soviets which was meeting at the time. The Bolshevik seizure of power marked the death of imperial Russia.

The imperial Russian state perished from its own weakness. During 1917 the apparatus of government disintegrated so that it was easy for the Bolsheviks, determined and convinced of their own mission, to take power from a demoralized and enfeebled Provisional Government. The reasons for this comprehensive collapse of the structures of the old regime were, however, rooted deeply in the history of the Russian state. For more than half a century, the Tsarist regime had proved unable to respond to calls for change with anything more than the most grudging acceptance of reform. In the wake of political reform in the 1860s and after 1905, the autocracy moved to try to reassert its authority and to negate the effects of the changes it had implemented but it could not, however, snuff out the sparks of autonomy that had been lit by the establishment of independent courts and local councils. Before 1905, the imperial Russian regime did not even pretend that it ruled with the consent of the empire's population: it believed that autocracy was the divinely ordained form of government for Russia. Even after 1905 and the establishment of a form of parliament, Nicholas II continued to believe that his autocratic power remained intact. The iron fist of Tsarism was rarely concealed by a velvet glove: coercion was a vital part of the state's armoury.

While these attitudes succeeded in keeping the regime in power, even though it was assailed by the assassination of Alexander II in 1881 and by revolution in 1905, they proved fatal in the long term. By persistently rejecting calls to allow the Russian public proper participation in government, successive Tsars ensured that the politically aware sections of Russian society became increasingly disenchanted with the autocracy. This disenchantment was, by 1914, turning to disengagement from the political process in any form. As the government moved further and further away from reform, the moderate politicians who had originally believed that the Duma offered a means for them to participate in the work of government became frustrated and alienated from the regime. The First World War brought these problems to a head, demonstrating the wholesale incompetence of Tsarism. The problems of Russia's political system were laid bare by the crisis of world war, but the real cause of the mess lay not in the war but in the very nature of the Russian autocracy.

The political vulnerability of the empire was made worse by its economic difficulties. Although Russian industrial growth was impressive during the 1890s, the structure of the economy remained essentially unchanged. The rural sector continued to dominate the Russian economy; it employed the overwhelming majority of the labour force and its output dwarfed that of other sectors of the economy. In 1861 and again in 1906 the state had acted to reform the structures of Russian agriculture, but neither the emancipation of the serfs nor the Stolypin land reform had succeeded in improving agricultural yields. This remained the bugbear of the Russian economy: a modernized industrial economy required an efficient agrarian sector which could produce sufficient food to support a large urban population. The Russian peasant economy, however, remained firmly orientated towards simply ensuring the subsistence of peasant farmers. The central concern of the peasantry remained land: peasant unrest in 1905 and during 1917 itself was aimed mainly at acquiring more land and thereby, the peasantry hoped, improving their fortunes. The state's attempts at agrarian reform did little to improve the condition of the peasant and peasant aspirations remained unsatisfied. The peasantry's traditional attachment to the Tsar weakened as it became clear that the state had no intention of granting them more land.

The industrial growth which Russia had experienced during the late nineteenth century proved barely adequate to support the state's ambitions. Russia remained far behind the other European powers in terms of industrial performance. In military terms, defeat in war in the Crimea the 1850s was repeated half a century later against Japan and in 1915 Russia was lucky not to suffer more comprehensive reverses. Without a prosperous industrial sector, the Russian government's ability to make social reform was severely limited, so that the conditions of life for working people in the burgeoning cities of the empire remained hard and unpleasant. While Western

European states, such as Britain and Germany, sought to deflect unrest by introducing measures such as old age pensions and insurance against unemployment, the Russian state remained both unwilling and unable to take such steps.

By the time war broke out in 1914, almost every section of Russian society felt betrayed by the autocracy. The peasantry, working people and the growing middle classes all felt that the political structures of the empire had failed to satisfy their needs. The sole bulwarks of Tsarist authority remained the landed nobility and the Orthodox Church, but the influence which these groups had on the mass of the population was declining. As so often, and as Germany and Austria-Hungary were to bear witness in 1918, war was the midwife of revolution. The First World War tested to the limit the ability of the Tsarist regime to deal with a crisis that engulfed the whole of Russian society. Even the nobility – the empire's traditional officer class – found their devotion to the Tsar weakened by the poor quality of top-level military decision-making. All the problems that had accumulated over the previous half-century came into sharp focus during the war. Poor military performance engendered even greater scepticism about the political capabilities of Tsarism. The unmodernized Russian economy was too weak to both supply the army and to maintain the standard of living of the peasantry and of working people. The government proved incapable of recognizing the strains which a war economy placed upon the ordinary people of the empire and failed to understand that it needed actively to win their support to ensure the success of the war effort. By 1917 the Russian people had no will to support either the person of the monarch, nor the system which he represented.

After February 1917, it became clear all too quickly that the problems which beset Russia could not be solved simply by the removal of the Tsar. The peoples of the Russian Empire had no enthusiasm for the institutions of his regime and were, instead, to experience the most radical change of government witnessed in Europe since 1789.

NOTES

1 THE POLITICS OF AUTOCRACY

1.   See D. Lieven, *Russia's Rulers under the Old Regime* (New Haven, 1989) and R. G. Robbins, *The Tsar's Viceroys* (Ithaca, 1987) for clear analysis of the political elite in both St Petersburg and the provinces.

2.   D. R. Brower, *Training the Nihilists* (Ithaca, 1975), p. 42.

3.   D. Lieven, *Nicholas II* (London, 1993), pp. 117–21, describes the consequences of this situation for the last Tsar.

4.   V. N. Kokovstov, *Iz moego proshlogo*, vol. 2 (Paris, 1933), pp. 278–9.

5.   H. W. Whelan, *Alexander III and the State Council. Bureaucracy and Counter-Reform in Late Imperial Russia* (New Brunswick, 1982), pp. 165–71.

6.   I. Blinov, *Gubernatory* (St Petersburg, 1905), p. 262.

7.   R. J. Abbott, 'Police Reform in the Russian Province of Iaroslavl, 1856–1876', *Slavic Review*, 32 (1973), p. 293.

8.   Rossiiskii Gosudarstvennyi Istoricheskii Arkhiv (Russian State Historical Archive; hereafter RGIA), f. 1276, op. 20, d. 52, l. 51. January 1912.

9.   P. Kalinin, 'Po povodu usilennoi okhrany', *Pravo* (10 February 1908), col. 316.

10. *Krasnyi Arkhiv*, 8 (1925), pp. 242–3.

11. A. V. Golovnin writing in 1863, quoted in M. K. Lemke, *Epokha tsenzurnykh reform 1859–1865 godov* (St Petersburg, 1904), p. 261.

12. K. L. Bermansky, '"Konstitutsionnye" proekty tsarstvovaniia Aleksandra II', *Vestnik Prava*, 35 (1905), p. 281.

13. D. Saunders, *Russia in the Age of Reaction and Reform 1801–1881* (Harlow, 1992), p. 156

14. J. Brooks, *When Russia Learned to Read. Literacy and Popular Literature, 1861–1917* (Princeton, 1985), pp. 61, 112.
15. P. L. Alston, 'The Dynamics of Educational Expansion in Russia', in K. H. Jarausch, *The Transformation of Higher Learning 1860–1930* (Chicago, 1983), pp. 89–92.
16. L. Tolstoy, *Anna Karenina* (Harmondsworth, 1954), pp. 677–94.
17. F. A. Petrov, 'Crowning the Edifice. The Zemstvo, Local Self-Government and the Constitutional Movement, 1864–1881', in B. Eklof, J. Bushnell and L. Zakharova, *Russia's Great Reforms, 1855–1881* (Bloomington, 1994), pp. 203–7.
18. S. Galai, *The Liberation Movement in Russia 1900–1905* (Cambridge, 1973), p. 20.
19. Saunders, *Russia in the Age of Reaction and Reform*, p. 336.
20. F. Venturi, *Roots of Revolution* (London, 1960), p. 665.
21. The text is in M. McCauley and P. Waldron, *The Emergence of the Modern Russian State 1855–1881* (London, 1988), pp. 142–4.
22. This peasant monarchism is well described in a different context in D. Field, *Rebels in the Name of the Tsar* (Boston, 1976).
23. Venturi, *Roots of Revolution*, p. 506.
24. R. Service, *Lenin: A Political Life*, vol. 1 (London, 1985), pp. 23–4.
25. J. L. H. Keep, *The Rise of Social Democracy in Russia* (Oxford, 1963), p. 21.
26. 'Dnevnik kn. Ekateriny Alekseevny Sviatopolk-Mirskoi za 1904–1905 gg', *Istoricheskie zapiski*, 77 (1965), p. 241.
27. T. Emmons, 'Russia's Banquet Campaign', *California Slavic Studies*, 10 (1977), pp. 45–86.
28. B. V. Anan'ich et al., *Krizis samoderzhaviia v Rossii 1895–1917* (Leningrad, 1984), p. 121.
29. *Pravo* (25 January 1904), col. 259.
30. G. T. Robinson, *Rural Russia under the Old Regime* (New York, 1932), p. 138.
31. See I. Nish, *The Origins of the Russo-Japanese War* (Harlow, 1985).
32. M. McCauley and P. Waldron (eds), *Octobrists to Bolsheviks* (London, 1984), p. 13.
33. A. Ascher, *The Revolution of 1905: Russia in Disarray* (Stanford, 1988), p. 94.
34. M. Perrie, 'The Russian Peasant Movement of 1905–7', in

B. Eklof and S.P. Frank (eds), *The World of the Russian Peasant: Post-Emancipation Culture and Society* (Boston MA, 1990), pp. 196–8.

35.   S. J. Seregny, 'Peasants and Politics: Peasant Unions During the 1905 Revolution', in E. Kingston-Mann and T. Mixter (eds), *Peasant Economy, Culture, and Politics of European Russia, 1800–1921* (Princeton, 1991), p. 348.

36.   RGIA, f. 1239, d. 1, l. 6.

37.   J. Bushnell, *Mutiny amid Repression. Russian Soldiers in the Revolution of 1905–1906* (Bloomington, 1985), p. 86.

38.   M. Szeftel, *The Russian Constitution of April 23, 1906* (Brussels, 1976) analyses the structure in detail.

39.   V. S. Diakin, *Samoderzhavie, burzhuaziia i dvorianstvo v 1907–1911gg.* (Leningrad, 1978), pp. 26–7.

40.   S. E. Kryzhanovskii, *Vospominaniia* (Berlin, 1925), ch. 4 is a description of the preparation of the new electoral law by its author, the assistant Minister of Internal Affairs.

41.   RGIA, f. 1288, op. 1, d. 29, l. 3.

42.   Speech by Stolypin to the Second Duma, 10 May 1907. *Gosudarstvennaia Duma. Stenograficheskie otchety.*, II, vol. 2, col. 349.

2 FIELD AND FACTORY: THE RUSSIAN ECONOMY

1.   P. Gregory, *Before Command. An Economic History of Russia from Emancipation to the First Five-Year Plan* (Princeton, 1994), pp. 17–22.

2.   D. Moon, 'Estimating the Peasant Population of Late Imperial Russia from the 1897 Census: A Research Note', *Europe-Asia Studies*, 48 (1996), pp. 141–53.

3.   G. Vernadsky et al. (eds), *A Source Book for Russian History from Early Times to 1917*, vol. 3 (New Haven, 1972), p. 589.

4.   D. M. Wallace, *Russia on the Eve of War and Revolution* (New York, 1961), p. 135.

5.   See O. Crisp, *Studies in the Russian Economy before 1914* (London, 1976), p. 82.

6.   J. Blum, *Lord and Peasant in Russia from the Ninth to the Nineteenth Century* (Princeton, 1961), p. 330 and R. Bideleux, 'Agricultural Advance Under the Russian Village Commune System', in R. Bartlett (ed.), *Land Commune and Peasant Community in Russia. Communal Forms in Imperial and Early*

Soviet Society (London 1990), pp. 210–11.

7. Iu. F. Samarin, 'O krepostnom sostoianii i o perekhode iz nego k grazhdanskoi svobode', *Sochineniia,* vol. 2 (Moscow, 1878), p. 19.

8. *Polnoe Sobranie Zakonov Rossiiskoi Imperii,* 2nd series, vol. 36, pt. 1, no. 36657.

9. S. L. Hoch, 'The Banking Crisis, Peasant Reform, and Economic Development in Russia, 1857–1861', *American Historical Review,* 96 (1991), pp. 810–11.

10. 'Saratovskii pomeshchik o khode reformy 19 fevralia 1861 g.', in I. A. Zhelvakova (ed.), *Revoliutsionnaia situatsiia v Rossii v 1859–1861 gg.* (Moscow, 1965), p. 451.

11. Robinson, *Rural Russia,* p. 290, note 24.

12. A. N. Engelgardt, *Iz derevni. 12 pisem 1872–87* (Moscow, 1960), p. 124.

13. H. T. Willetts, 'The Agrarian Problem', in G. Katkov et al. (eds), *Russia Enters the Twentieth Century* (London, 1971), p. 126.

14. D. A. J. Macey, 'Government Actions and Peasant Reactions During the Stolypin Reforms', in R. B. McKean (ed.), *New Perspectives in Modern Russian History* (London, 1992), p. 154.

15. J. Pallot, 'Did the Stolypin Land Reform Destroy the Peasant Commune?', in McKean, *New Perspectives,* p. 129.

16. O. Crisp, 'Labour and Industrialization in Russia', in P. Mathias and M. M. Postan (eds), *Cambridge Economic History of Europe,* vol. VII, pt. 2 (Cambridge, 1978), pp. 364, 371.

17. A. P. Korelin, *Dvorianstvo v poreformennoi Rossii, 1861–1904* (Moscow, 1979), p. 57 and P. Gatrell, *The Tsarist Economy 1850–1917* (London, 1986), p. 114.

18. Robinson, *Rural Russia,* p. 101.

19. S. G. Wheatcroft, 'Crises and the Condition of the Peasantry in Late Imperial Russia', in E. Kingston-Mann and T. Mixter, *Peasant Economy,* pp. 133–5.

20. S. G. Wheatcroft, 'The 1891–92 Famine in Russia: Towards a More Detailed Analysis of its Scale and Demographic Significance', in L. Edmondson and P. Waldron (eds), *Economy and Society in Russia and the Soviet Union, 1860–1930* (London, 1992), p. 47.

21. B. N. Chicherin, *Vospominaniia. Zemstvo i Moskovskaia Duma* (Moscow, 1934), p. 60.

22. L. Volin, *A Century of Russian Agriculture: From Alexander II to Khrushchev* (Cambridge MA, 1970), p. 59.

23. *Materialy dlia geografii i statistiki Rossii, sobrannye ofitserami generalnogo shtaba. Riazanskaia guberniia* (St Petersburg, 1860), p. 400.
24. Crisp, 'Labour and Industrialization in Russia', p. 324.
25. Gatrell, *The Tsarist Economy*, pp. 110–11.
26. Wheatcroft, 'Crises', pp. 151–3.
27. Wheatcroft, 'Crises', pp. 144–5.
28. Gregory, *Before Command*, p. 48.
29. Wheatcroft, 'Crises', p. 159.
30. D. Christian, *Living Water. Vodka and Russian Society on the Eve of Emancipation* (Oxford, 1990), pp. 372–3.
31. Gatrell, *The Tsarist Economy*, p. 220.
32. Crisp, *Studies*, p. 13.
33. Gatrell, *The Tsarist Economy*, pp. 166–7.
34. Crisp, *Studies*, pp. 25–6.
35. S. G. Marks, *Road to Power. The Trans-Siberian Railroad and the Colonization of Asian Russia, 1850–1917* (Ithaca, 1991), p. 150.
36. P. Gregory, *Russian National Income, 1885–1913* (Cambridge, 1982), p. 252.
37. J. P. McKay, *Pioneers for Profit. Foreign Entrepreneurship and Russian Industrialization 1885–1913* (Chicago, 1970), pp. 26–8.
38. Crisp, *Studies*, p. 48.

3 THE TRANSFORMATION OF RUSSIAN SOCIETY

1. W. G. Wagner, *Marriage, Property and Law in Late Imperial Russia* (Oxford, 1994), p. 229.
2. C. Worobec, *Peasant Russia. Family and Community in the Post-Emancipation Period* (Princeton, 1991), p. 185.
3. See A. Martynova, 'Life of the Pre-Revolutionary Village as Reflected in Popular Lullabies', in D. L. Ransel (ed.), *The Family in Imperial Russia. New Lines of Historical Research* (Urbana, 1978), pp. 171–85.
4. Worobec, *Peasant Russia*, p. 128.
5. O. S. Tian-Shanskaia, *Village Life in Late Tsarist Russia* (Bloomington, 1993), p. 63.
6. S. C. Ramer, 'Childbirth and Culture: Midwifery in the Nineteenth-Century Russian Countryside', in Ransel (ed.), *The Family*, p. 218.

7. J. Bradley, *Muzhik and Muscovite. Urbanization in Late Imperial Russia* (Berkeley, 1985), p. 219.

8. The term is used by R. E. Johnson in *Peasant and Proletarian: The Working Class of Moscow in the Late Nineteenth Century* (New Brunswick, 1979).

9. Bradley, *Muzhik*, p. 222.

10. R. Stites, *The Women's Liberation Movement in Russia* (Princeton, 1978), p. 83.

11. L. H. Edmondson, *Feminism in Russia, 1900–17* (London, 1984), p. 87.

12. A. G. Meyer, 'The Impact of World War I on Russian Women's Lives', in B. E. Clements, B. A. Engel and C. D. Worobec (eds), *Russia's Women* (Berkeley, 1991), p. 214.

13. D. Atkinson, *The End of the Russian Land Commune 1905–1930* (Stanford, 1983), p. 4.

14. Wallace, *Russia*, p. 351.

15. A. Chekhov, 'Peasants', in *The Russian Master and other Stories*, trans. R. Hingley (Oxford, 1984), p. 162.

16. B. Mironov, 'The Peasant Commune after the Reforms of the 1860s', *Slavic Review*, 44 (1985), p. 449.

17. *Sbornik materialov dlia izucheniia selskoi pozemelnoi obshchiny*, vol. 1 (St Petersburg, 1880), p. 168.

18. E. Kingston-Mann, 'Peasant Communes and Economic Innovation: A Preliminary Inquiry', in Kingston-Mann and Mixter (eds), *Peasant Economy*, p. 43.

19. Atkinson, *The End*, p. 83.

20. A. N. Engelgardt, *Letters from the Country, 1872–1887*, trans. and ed. C. A. Frierson (Oxford, 1993), p. 48.

21. J. S. Curtiss, *Church and State in Russia: The Last Years of the Empire* (New York, 1940), pp. 74–5.

22. G. L. Freeze, 'Handmaiden of the State? The Church in Imperial Russia Reconsidered', *Journal of Ecclesiastical History*, 36 (1985), p. 98.

23. See P. Waldron, 'Religious Reform after 1905: Old Believers and the Orthodox Church', *Oxford Slavonic Papers*, New Series, 20 (1987), pp. 110–39.

24. D. W. Treadgold, *The Great Siberian Migration* (Princeton, 1957), p. 34.

25. V. E. Bonnell (ed.), *The Russian Worker. Life and Labor under the Tsarist Regime* (Berkeley, 1983), pp. 47–8.

26. M. Engman, 'The Finns in St Petersburg', in M. Engman

et al. (eds), *Ethnic Identity in Urban Europe. Comparative Studies on Governments and Non-Dominant Ethnic Groups in Europe, 1850–1940, vol. VIII* (Aldershot, 1992), p. 103.

27.   Gosudarstvennaia Duma, *Stenograficheskie otchety*, III (IV), vol. 11, cols 98–9.

28.   Bradley, *Muzhik*, p. 303.

29.   R. B. McKean, *St. Petersburg Between the Revolutions. Workers and Revolutionaries June 1907–February 1917* (New Haven, 1990), p. 67.

30.   A. N. Anfimov, *Krupnoe pomeshchishchee khoziaistvo Evropeiskoi Rossii* (Moscow, 1969), p. 275.

31.   A. P. Korelin, *Dvorianstvo v poreformennoi Rossii 1861–1904gg.* (Moscow, 1979), p. 54.

32.   R. T. Manning, *The Crisis of the Old Order in Russia. Gentry and Government* (Princeton, 1982), p. 10.

33.   S. Becker, *Nobility and Privilege in Late Imperial Russia* (DeKalb, 1985), p. 115.

34.   Korelin, *Dvorianstvo*, p. 94.

35.   G. A. Hosking and R. T. Manning, 'What Was the United Nobility?', in L. H. Haimson (ed.), *The Politics of Rural Russia 1905–1914* (Bloomington, 1979), p. 147.

36.   See *Trudy pervogo s"ezda upolnomochennykh dvorianskikh obshchestv 21–28.5.06* (St Petersburg, 1906), pp. 105–8 for the congress's initial resolution.

37.   V. R. Leikina-Svirskaia, *Russkaia intelligentsia v 1900–1917 godakh* (Moscow, 1981), pp. 47–60.

38.   A. J. Rieber, *Merchants and Entrepreneurs in Imperial Russia* (Chapel Hill, 1982), pp. 420–1.

39.   H. Balzer, 'The Problem of Professions in Imperial Russia', in E. W. Clowes, S. D. Kassow and J. L. West (eds), *Between Tsar and People* (Princeton, 1991), p. 189.

40.   P. Waldron, 'States of Emergency: Autocracy and Emergency Legislation, 1881–1917', *Revolutionary Russia*, 8 (1995), p. 10.

41.   V. Ia. Laverychev, *Krupnaia burzhuaziia v poreformennoi Rossii (1861–1900gg.)* (Moscow, 1974), pp. 204–5.

42.   J. Brooks, 'Readers and Reading at the End of the Tsarist Era', in W. M. Todd III (ed.), *Literature and Society in Imperial Russia, 1800–1914* (Stanford, 1978), p. 115.

43.   B. Eklof, *Russian Peasant Schools. Officialdom, Village Culture and Popular Pedagogy, 1861–1914* (Berkeley, 1986), p. 90.

44.   A. M. Gudvan, 'Essays on the History of the Movement of

Sales-Clerical Workers in Russia', in Bonnell (ed.), *The Russian Worker*, p. 208.
45. G. H. N. Seton-Watson, *The Russian Empire 1801–1917* (Oxford, 1967), p. 476.
46. Quoted in '"Vozhd" reaktsii 60–80-kh godov', *Byloe* (1917), no. 4, p. 6.
47. Alston, 'The Dynamics of Educational Expansion', p. 96.
48. A. G. Rashin, *Naseleniia Rossii za sto let (1811–1913 gg.)* (Moscow, 1956), pp. 309–10.
49. J. Brooks, *When Russia Learned to Read. Literacy and Popular Literature, 1861–1917* (Princeton, 1985), p. 112.
50. M. E. Saltykov-Shchedrin, 'Ulichnaia filosofiia', in *Sobranie sochinenii*, vol. 9 (Moscow, 1970), pp. 62–3.
51. V. V. Stasov, 'Dvadtsat' piat' let russkogo isskustva', *Vestnik Evropy*, 98 (1882), p. 254.

4 EMPIRE AND EUROPE

1. Quoted in S. S. Tatishchev, *Imperator Aleksandr II: Ego zhizn' i tsarstvovanie*, vol. 2 (St Petersburg, 1903), p. 115.
2. *Zapiska o znachenii Bukharskogo khanstva dlia Rossii i neobkhodimosti priniatiia reshiltel'nykh mer dlia prochnogo vodvoreniia nashego vliianiia v Srednoi Azii* (St Petersburg, 1867), p. 38.
3. *Vosstanie 1916-ogo goda v Srednei Azii i Kazakhstane* (Moscow, 1960), p. 68.
4. R. E. Blobaum, *Rewolucja. Russian Poland, 1904–1907* (Ithaca, 1995), pp. 33–4.
5. D. G. Kirby (ed.), *Finland and Russia 1808–1920. From Autonomy to Independence* (London, 1975), p. 57.
6. O. Subtelny, *Ukraine: A History* (Toronto, 1988), p. 282.
7. Lieven, *Russia's Rulers*, p. 32.
8. J. W. Long, *From Privilege to Dispossessed. The Volga Germans, 1860–1917* (Lincoln NE, 1988), p. 197.
9. C. Gassenschmidt, *Liberal Jewish Politics in Tsarist Russia, 1900–1914* (London, 1995), pp. 21–3.
10. A. Walicki, *A History of Russian Thought From the Enlightenment to Marxism* (Stanford, 1979), p. 297.
11. J. D. Morison, 'Katkov and Panslavism', *Slavonic and East European Review*, 46 (1968), p. 423.

12.   E. C. Thaden, 'The Russian Government', in E. C. Thaden (ed.), *Russification in the Baltic Provinces and Finland, 1855–1914* (Princeton, 1981), pp. 44–5.

13.   P. N. Maikov, *Finliandiia, ee proshedshee i nastoiashchee* (St Petersburg, 1905), p. 525.

14.   T. Polvinen, *Imperial Borderland. Bobrikov and the Attempted Russification of Finland 1898–1904* (London, 1995), p. 71.

15.   The text of the edict is in McCauley and Waldron, *The Emergence of the Modern Russian State*, p. 209.

16.   P. A. Zaionchkovskii, *Krizis samoderzhaviia na rubezhe 1870–1880 godov* (Moscow, 1964), pp. 71–2.

17.   G. Freeze (ed.), *From Supplication to Revolution. A Documentary Social History of Imperial Russia* (New York, 1988), p. 300.

18.   H. D. Mehlinger and J. M. Thompson, *Count Witte and the Tsarist Government in the 1905 Revolution* (Bloomington, 1972), p. 227.

19.   N. P. Ignatev, 'Zapiski', *Istoricheskii Vestnik*, 135 (1914), p. 54.

20.   M. B. Petrovich, *The Emergence of Russian Panslavism, 1856–1870* (New York, 1956), p. 201.

21.   E. C. Thaden, *Conservative Nationalism in 19th Century Russia* (Seattle, 1964), p. 146.

22.   D. Geyer, *Russian Imperialism. The Interaction of Domestic and Foreign Policy 1860–1914* (Leamington Spa, 1987), p. 107.

23.   B. W. Menning, *Bayonets before Bullets. The Imperial Russian Army, 1861–1914* (Bloomington, 1992), p. 22

24.   W. C. Fuller, *Strategy and Power in Russia 1600–1914* (New York, 1992), p. 324.

25.   McCauley and Waldron, *The Emergence of the Modern Russian State*, p. 165.

26.   D. MacKenzie, 'Russia's Balkan policies under Alexander II, 1855–1881', in H. Ragsdale (ed.), *Imperial Russian Foreign Policy* (Cambridge, 1993), p. 228.

27.   A. J. P. Taylor, *The Struggle for Mastery in Europe 1848–1918* (Oxford, 1954), p. 261.

28.   Geyer, *Russian Imperialism*, p. 156.

29.   Quoted in Fuller, *Strategy and Power*, p. 415.

30.   See D. M. McDonald, *United Government and Foreign Policy in Russia, 1900–1914* (Cambridge MA, 1992).

31.   D. C. B. Lieven, *Russia and the Origins of the First World War* (London, 1983), p. 45.

32.   S. D. Sazonov, *Vospominaniia* (Paris, 1927), p. 182.

33.   Lieven, *Russia and the Origins*, p. 144.

5 THE END OF THE OLD ORDER

1. McCauley and Waldron, *From Octobrists to Bolsheviks*, p. 66.
2. Quoted in F. A. Golder (ed.), *Documents of Russian History 1914–1917* (New York, 1927), p. 19.
3. N. Stone, *The Eastern Front 1914–1917* (London, 1975), p. 191.
4. Fuller, *Strategy and Power*, p. 450.
5. McKean, *St. Petersburg Between the Revolutions*, p. 320.
6. A. L. Sidorov, *Ekonomicheskoe polozhenie Rossii v gody pervoi mirovoi voiny* (Moscow, 1973), p. 12.
7. L. Siegelbaum, 'Moscow Industrialists during World War I', *Russian History*, 5, pt. 1 (1978), p. 71.
8. Gatrell, *The Tsarist Economy*, p. 185.
9. A. N. Antsiferov et al., *Russian Agriculture during the War* (New Haven, 1930), p. 132.
10. A. N. Anfimov, *Rossiiskaia derevnia v gody pervoi mirovoi voiny* (Moscow, 1962), p. 293.
11. McKean, *St. Petersburg Between the Revolutions*, p. 345.
12. R. Pearson, *The Russian Moderates and the Crisis of Tsarism 1914–1917* (London, 1977), p. 20.
13. P. P. Gronsky and N. J. Astrov, *The War and the Russian Government* (New Haven, 1929), p. 192.
14. *Krasnyi Arkhiv*, 50 (1932), p. 133.
15. M. Cherniavsky (ed.), *Prologue to Revolution* (Englewood Cliffs, 1967), pp. 226–7.
16. B. Pares (ed.), *The Letters of the Tsaritsa to the Tsar, 1914–1916* (London, 1923), p. 394.
17. Gosudarstvennaia Duma, *Stenograficheskie otchety*, IV (V), col. 48.
18. A. K. Wildman, *The End of the Russian Imperial Army. The Old Army and the Soldiers' Revolt (March–April 1917)* (Princeton, 1980), pp. 77–8.
19. *Krasnyi Arkhiv*, 17 (1926), p. 20
20. *Krest'ianskoe dvizhenie v Rossii v 1914–1917gg.* (Moscow–Leningrad, 1965), pp. 513–14.
21. McKean, *St. Petersburg Between the Revolutions*, p. 336.
22. D. Koenker, *Moscow Workers and the 1917 Revolution* (Princeton, 1981), p. 86.
23. T. Hasegawa, *The February Revolution. Petrograd 1917* (Seattle 1981), p. 275.

24. M. Perrie, 'The Peasants', in R. Service (ed.), *Society and Politics in the Russian Revolution* (London, 1992), p. 16.
25. Koenker, *Moscow Workers*, p. 295.
26. Figures are very difficult to verify as indicated in R. Service, *The Bolshevik Party in Revolution 1917–1923* (London, 1979), pp. 42–3.

SELECT BIBLIOGRAPHY

General Works

Channon, J. and Hudson, R. *The Penguin Historical Atlas of Russia* (Harmondsworth, 1995).

Freeze, G. *From Supplication to Revolution. A Documentary Social History of Imperial Russia* (New York, 1988).

Gooding, J. *Rulers and Subjects. Government and People in Russia 1801–1991* (London, 1996).

McCauley, M. and Waldron, P. *Octobrists to Bolsheviks. Imperial Russia 1905–1917* (London, 1984).

—— *The Emergence of the Modern Russian State, 1855–1881* (London, 1988).

Pipes, R. *Russia under the Old Regime* (London, 1974).

—— *The Russian Revolution 1899–1919* (London, 1990).

Rogger, H. *Russia in the Age of Modernisation and Revolution 1881–1917* (Harlow, 1983).

Saunders, D. *Russia in the Age of Reaction and Reform 1801–1881* (Harlow, 1992).

Service, R. *The Russian Revolution 1900–1927* (London, 1986).

Seton-Watson, H. *The Russian Empire 1801–1917* (Oxford, 1967).

Politics

Ascher, A. *Pavel Axelrod and the Development of Menshevism* (Cambridge MA, 1972).

—— *The Revolution of 1905*, 2 vols, (Stanford, 1988 and 1992).

Badayev, A. Y. *Bolsheviks in the Tsarist Duma* (London, 1987).

Balmuth, D. *Censorship in Russia, 1865–1905* (Washington DC, 1979).

Choldin, M. T. *A Fence round the Empire. Russian Censorship of Western Ideas under the Tsars* (Durham NC, 1985).

Christoff, P. K. *K. S. Aksakov. A Study in Ideas* (Princeton, 1982).

Deutscher, I. *The Prophet Armed. Trotsky: 1879–1921* (Oxford, 1954).

Edelman, R. *Gentry Politics on the Eve of the Russian Revolution. The Nationalist Party 1907–1917* (New Brunswick, 1980).

—— *Proletarian Peasants. The Revolution of 1905 in Russia's Southwest* (Ithaca, 1987).

Eklof, B., Bushnell, J. and Zakharova, L. (eds) *Russia's Great Reforms, 1855–1881* (Bloomington, 1994).

Emmons, T. *The Formation of Political Parties and the First National Elections in Russia* (Cambridge MA, 1983).

Emmons, T. (ed.) *The Zemstvo in Russia: An Experiment in Local Self-Government* (Cambridge, 1982).

Fröhlich, K. *The Emergence of Russian Constitutionalism 1900–1904* (The Hague, 1981).

Fuller, W. C. *Civil–Military Conflict in Imperial Russia 1881–1914* (Princeton, 1985).

Galai, S. *The Liberation Movement in Russia, 1900–1905* (Cambridge, 1973).

Geifman, A. *Thou Shalt Kill. Revolutionary Terorism in Russia, 1894–1917* (Princeton, 1993).

Gleason, A. *Young Russia. The Genesis of Russian Radicalism in the 1860s* (New York, 1980).

Haimson, L. H. (ed.) *The Politics of Rural Russia 1905–1914* (Bloomington, 1979).

Hamburg, G. *The Politics of the Russian Nobility, 1881–1905* (New Brunswick, 1984).

Harcave, S. (trans. and ed.) *The Memoirs of Count Witte. A Portrait of the Twilight Years of Tsarism by the Man who Built Modern Russia* (London, 1990).

Harding, N. *Lenin's Political Thought* (2 vols, London, 1977 and 1981).

Hardy, D. *Land and Freedom. The Origins of Russian Terrorism 1876–1879* (Westport, 1987).

Hosking, G. A. *The Russian Constitutional Experiment. Government and Duma 1907–1914* (Cambridge, 1973).

Judge, E. H. *Plehve. Repression and Reform in Imperial Russia 1902–1904* (Syracuse, 1983).

Keep, J. L. H. *The Rise of Social Democracy in Russia* (Oxford, 1963).

Lieven, D. *Russia's Rulers under the Old Regime* (New Haven, 1989).

—— *Nicholas II* (London 1993).

Lincoln, W. B. *Nikolai Miliutin. An Enlightened Russian Bureaucrat* (Newtonville, 1977).

—— *In the Vanguard of Reform. Russia's Enlightened Bureaucrats 1825–1861* (DeKalb, 1982).

—— *The Great Reforms: Autocracy, Bureaucracy and the Politics of Change in Imperial Russia* (DeKalb, 1990).

Manning, R. T. *The Crisis of the Old Order in Russia. Gentry and Government* (Princeton, 1982).

McDaniel, T. *Autocracy, Capitalism and Revolution in Russia* (Berkeley, 1988).

Mehlinger, H. D. and Thompson, J. M. *Count Witte and the Tsarist Government in the 1905 Revolution* (Bloomington, 1972).

Melancon, M. *The Socialist Revolutionaries and the Russian Anti-War Movement, 1914–1917* (Columbus, 1990).

Miller, F. A. *Dmitrii Miliutin and the Reform Era in Russia* (Vanderbilt, 1968).

Miller, M. A. *Kropotkin* (Chicago, 1976).

Naimark, N. *Terrorists and Social Democrats. The Russian Revolutionary Movement under Alexander III* (Cambridge, 1983).

Offord, D. *The Russian Revolutionary Movement in the 1880s* (Cambridge, 1986).

Orlovsky, D. T. *The Limits of Reform. The Ministry of Internal Affairs in Imperial Russia, 1801–1881* (Cambridge, 1981).

Pearson, R. *The Russian Moderates and the Crisis of Tsarism 1914–1917* (London, 1977).

Pearson, T. S. *Russian Officialdom in Crisis: Autocracy and Local Self-Government, 1861–1900* (Cambridge, 1989).

Pereira, N. G. O. *Tsar-Liberator: Alexander II of Russia 1818–1881* (Newtonville, 1983).

Perrie, M. *The Agrarian Policy of the Russian Socialist-Revolutionary Party from its Origins through the Revolution of 1905–1907* (Cambridge, 1976).

Pinchuk, B.-C. *The Octobrists in the Third Duma, 1907 1912* (Seattle, 1974).

Pintner, W. M. and Rowney, D. K. *Russian Officialdom: The Bureaucratization of Russian Society from the Seventeenth to the Twentieth Century* (London, 1980).

Pomper, P. *Peter Lavrov and the Russian Revolutionary Movement* (Chicago, 1972).

—— *Sergei Nechaev* (New Brunswick, 1979).

Rawson, D. C. *Russian Rightists and the Revolution of 1905* (Cambridge, 1995).

Robbins, R. G. *The Tsar's Viceroys. Russian Provincial Governors in the Last Years of the Empire* (Ithaca, 1987).

Sablinsky, W. *The Road to Bloody Sunday. The Role of Father Gapon* and the Assembly of Russian Factory Workers in the Petersburg Massacre of 1905 (Princeton, 1976).

Schneiderman, J. *Sergei Zubatov and Revolutionary Marxism. The Struggle for the Working Class in Tsarist Russia* (Ithaca, 1976).

Service, R. *Lenin: A Political Life*, 3 vols (London, 1985, 1991 and 1994).

Starr, S. F. *Decentralization and Self-Government in Russia, 1830–1870* (Princeton, 1972).

Swain, G. *Russian Social-Democracy and the Legal Labour Movement, 1906–1914* (London, 1983).

Szeftel, M. *The Russian Constitution of April 23, 1906. Political Institutions of the Duma Monarchy* (Brussels, 1976).

Thaden, E. C. *Conservative Nationalism in Nineteenth-Century Russia* (Seattle, 1964).

Venturi, F. *Roots of Revolution. A History of the Populist and Socialist Movements in Nineteenth-Century Russia* (London, 1960).

Verner, A. M. *The Crisis of Russian Autocracy. Nicholas II and the 1905 Revolution* (Princeton, 1990).

Wcislo, F. W. *Reforming Rural Russia. State, Local Society and National Politics 1855–1914* (Princeton, 1990).

Weissman, N. B. *Reform in Tsarist Russia. The State Bureaucracy and Local Government, 1900–1914* (New Brunswick, 1981).

Whelan, H. W. *Alexander III and the State Council. Bureaucracy and Counter-Reform in Late Imperial Russia* (New Brunswick, 1982).

Wortman, R. *The Crisis of Russian Populism* (Cambridge, 1967).

—— *The Development of a Russian Legal Consciousness* (Chicago, 1976).

Yaney, G. L. *The Systematization of Russian Government: Social Evolution in the Domestic Administration of Imperial Russia 1711–1905* (Urbana, 1973).

—— *The Urge to Mobilize. Agrarian Reform in Russia, 1861–1930* (Urbana, 1982).

Zaionchkovskii, P. A. *The Russian Autocracy under Alexander III* (Gulf Breeze, 1976).

—— *The Abolition of Serfdom in Russia* (Gulf Breeze, 1978).

—— *The Russian Autocracy in Crisis, 1878–1882* (Gulf Breeze, 1979).

The Economy

Bartlett, R. (ed.) *Land Commune and Peasant Community in Russia. Communal Forms in Imperial and Early Soviet Society* (London, 1990).

Crisp, O. *Studies in the Russian Economy before 1914* (London, 1976).

—— 'Labour and Industrialization in Russia', in P. Mathias and M. M. Postan (eds), *The Cambridge Economic History of Europe*, vol. VII, pt. 2 (Cambridge, 1978).

Edmondson, L. and Waldron, P. (eds) *Economy and Society in Russia and the Soviet Union, 1860–1930* (London, 1992).

Falkus, M. E. *The Industrialization of Russia 1700–1914* (London, 1970).

Gatrell, P. *The Tsarist Economy 1850–1917* (London, 1986).

—— *Government, Industry and Rearmament in Russia, 1900–1914. The Last Argument of Tsarism* (Cambridge, 1994).

Gerschenkron, A. *Economic Backwardness in Historical Perspective* (Cambridge MA, 1962).

—— 'Agrarian Policies and Industrialization: Russia 1861–1917', in P. Mathias and M. M. Postan (eds), *The Cambridge Economic History of Europe*, vol. 6, pt. 2 (Cambridge, 1966).

Gregory, P. *Russian National Income, 1885–1913* (Cambridge, 1982).

—— *Before Command. An Economic History of Russia from Emancipation to the First Five-Year Plan* (Princeton, 1994).

Kahan, A. *Russian Economic History. The Nineteenth Century* (Chicago, 1989).

McKay, J. P. *Pioneers for Profit. Foreign Entrepreneurship and Russian Industrialization 1885–1913* (Chicago, 1970).

Robbins, R. G. *Famine in Russia 1891–1892. The Imperial Government Responds to a Crisis* (New York, 1975).

Robinson, G. T. *Rural Russia under the Old Regime* (New York, 1932).

Simms, J. Y. 'The Crisis in Russian Agriculture at the End of the Nineteenth Century: A Different View', *Slavic Review*, 36 (1977), pp. 377–98.

Von Laue, T. H. *Sergei Witte and the Industrialization of Russia* (New York, 1963).

Society

Atkinson, D. *The End of the Russian Land Commune, 1903–1930* (Stanford, 1983).

Balzer, M. M. (ed.) *Russian Traditional Culture: Religion, Gender and Customary Law* (Armonk, 1992).

Bater, J. H. *St. Petersburg: Industrialization and Change* (London, 1976).

Becker, S. *Nobility and Privilege in Late Imperial Russia* (DeKalb, 1985).

Bonnell, V. E. *Roots of Rebellion. Workers' Politics and Organizations in St. Petersburg and Moscow, 1900–1914* (Berkeley, 1983).

Bonnell, V. E. (ed.) *The Russian Worker. Life and Labor under the Tsarist Regime* (Berkeley, 1983).

Bradley, J. *Muzhik and Muscovite. Urbanization in Late Imperial Russia* (Berkeley, 1985).

Brooks, J. *When Russia Learned to Read. Literacy and Popular Literature, 1861–1917* (Princeton, 1985).

Brower, D. *The Russian City between Tradition and Modernity, 1850–1900* (Berkeley, 1990).

Bushnell, J. *Mutiny amid Repression. Russian Soldiers in the Revolution of 1905–1906* (Bloomington, 1985).

Christian, D. *Living Water. Vodka and Russian Society on the Eve of Emancipation* (Oxford, 1990).

Clements, B. E., Engel, B. A. and Worobec, C. D. (eds) *Russia's Women* (Berkeley, 1991).

Clowes, E. W., Kassow, S. D. and West, J. L. (eds) *Between Tsar and People. Educated Society and the Quest for Public Identity in Late Imperial Russia* (Princeton, 1991).

Crisp, O. and Edmondson, L. (eds) *Civil Rights in Imperial Russia* (Oxford, 1989).

Curtiss, J. S. *Church and State in Russia. The Last Years of the Empire, 1900–1917* (New York, 1940).

Edmondson, L. H. *Feminism in Russia, 1900–1917* (London, 1984).

Eklof, B. *Russian Peasant Schools. Officialdom, Village Culture, and Popular Pedagogy, 1861–1914* (Berkeley, 1986).

Eklof, B. and Frank, S. P. *The World of the Russian Peasant. Post-Emancipation Culture and Society* (Boston MA, 1990).

Emmons, T. *The Russian Gentry and the Peasant Emancipation of 1861* (Cambridge, 1968).

Engel, B. A. *Mothers and Daughters: Women of the Intelligentsia in Nineteenth-Century Russia* (Cambridge, 1983).

—— *Between the Field and the City. Women, Work and Family in Russia, 1861–1914* (Cambridge, 1994).

Engelstein, L. *Moscow, 1905. Working-class Organization and Political Conflict* (Stanford, 1982).

Farnsworth, B. and Viola, L. (eds) *Russian Peasant Women* (New York, 1992).

Field, D. *The End of Serfdom. Nobility and Bureaucracy in Russia, 1855–1861* (Cambridge, 1976).

—— *Rebels in the Name of the Tsar* (Boston, 1976).

Freeze, G. *The Parish Clergy in Nineteenth Century Russia. Crisis, Reform, Counter-Reform* (Princeton, 1983).

—— 'The *Soslovie* (Estate) Paradigm and Russian Social History', *American Historical Review*, 91 (1986), pp. 11–36.

Frieden, N. M. *Russian Physicians in an Era of Reform and Revolution, 1865–1905* (Princeton, 1981).

Frierson, C. A. *Peasant Icons. Representations of Rural People in Late 19th Century Russia* (New York, 1993).

Glickman, R. *Russian Factory Women. Workplace and Society, 1880–1914* (Berkeley, 1984).

Haberer, E. *Jews and Revolution in Nineteenth-century Russia* (Cambridge, 1985).

Haimson, L. 'The Problem of Urban Stability in Russia, 1905–1917', *Slavic Review*, 23 (1964), pt. 4, and 24 (1965), pt. 1.

Hamm, M. F. (ed.) *The City in Late Imperial Russia* (Bloomington, 1986).

Johnson, R. E. *Peasant and Proletarian. The Working Class of Moscow in the Late Nineteenth Century* (New Brunswick, 1979).

Kassow, S. D. *Students, Professors and the State in Tsarist Russia* (Berkeley, 1989).

Kinston-Mann, E. and Mixter, T. *Peasant Economy, Culture and Politics of European Russia, 1800–1921* (Princeton, 1991).

McClelland, J. C. *Autocrats and Academics. Education, Culture and Society in Tsarist Russia* (Chicago, 1979).

McKean, R. *St. Petersburg Between the Revolutions. Workers and Revolutionaries June 1907–February 1917* (New Haven, 1990).

Neuberger, J. *Hooliganism: Crime, Culture and Power in St Petersburg 1900–1914* (Berkeley, 1993).

Nichols, R. L. and Stavrou, T. G. *Russian Orthodoxy under the Old Regime* (Minneapolis, 1978).

Owen, T. C. *Capitalism and Politics in Russia: A Social History of the Moscow Merchants 1855–1905* (Cambridge, 1981).

Ransel, D. (ed.) *The Family in Imperial Russia. New Lines of Historical Research* (Urbana, 1978).

Read, C. *Religion, Revolution and the Russian Intelligentsia* (London, 1979).

Rieber, A. J. *Merchants and Entrepreneurs in Imperial Russia* (Chapel Hill, 1982).

Ruckman, J. A. *The Moscow Business Elite. A Social and Cultural Portrait of Two Generations* (DeKalb, 1984).

Seregny, S. *Russian Teachers and Peasant Revolution. The Politics of*

Education in 1905 (Bloomington, 1989).

Stavrou, T. G. (ed.) *Art and Culture in Nineteenth-Century Russia* (Bloomington, 1983).

Stites, R. *The Women's Liberation Movement in Russia* (Princeton, 1978).

Thurston, R. W. *Liberal City, Conservative State. Moscow and Russia's Urban Crisis, 1906–1914* (Oxford, 1987).

Tian-Shanskaia, O. S. *Village Life in Late Tsarist Russia* (Bloomington, 1993).

Treadgold, D. W. *The Great Siberian Migration* (Princeton, 1957).

Vucinich, W. S. (ed.) *The Peasant in Nineteenth-Century Russia* (Stanford, 1968).

Wagner, W. G. *Marriage, Property and Law in Late Imperial Russia* (Oxford, 1994).

Worobec, C. D. *Peasant Russia. Family and Community in the Post-Emancipation Era* (Princeton, 1991).

Nationalities, Foreign Policy and the Army

Allworth, E. (ed.) *Central Asia: 120 Years of Russian Rule* (Durham NC, 1989).

Aronson, I. M. *Troubled Waters: The Origins of the 1881 Anti-Jewish Pogroms in Russia* (Pittsburgh, 1990).

Becker, S. *Russia's Protectorates in Central Asia: Bukhara and Khiva, 1865–1924* (Cambridge MA, 1968).

Blobaum, R. E. *Rewolucja. Russian Poland, 1904–1907* (Ithaca, 1995).

Curtiss, J. S. *Russia's Crimean War* (Durham NC, 1979).

Forsyth, J. *A History of the Peoples of Siberia. Russia's North Asian Colony* (Cambridge, 1992).

Fuller, W. C. *Strategy and Power in Russia 1600–1914* (New York, 1992).

Geyer, D. *Russian Imperialism. The Interaction of Domestic and Foreign Policy, 1860–1914* (Leamington Spa, 1987).

Goldfrank, D. M. *The Origins of the Crimean War* (London, 1994).

Henriksson, A. *The Tsar's Loyal Germans. The Riga German Community: Social Change and the Nationality Question, 1855–1905* (Boulder, 1983).

Jelavich, B. *Tsarist Russia and Balkan Nationalism, 1879–1886* (Berkeley, 1962).

Keep, J. L. H. *Soldiers of the Tsar: Army and Society in Russia 1462–1874* (Oxford, 1985).

Kennan, G. F. *The Fateful Alliance. France, Russia and the Coming of the First World War* (New York, 1984).

Kirby, D. *The Baltic World 1772–1993* (Harlow, 1995).

Kirby, D. G. (ed.) *Finland and Russia 1808–1920. From Autonomy to Independence* (London, 1975).

Klier, J. D. *Imperial Russia's Jewish Question, 1855–1881* (Cambridge, 1995).

Lieven, D. C. B. *Russia and the Origins of the First World War* (London, 1983).

Long, J. W. *From Privileged to Dispossessed. The Volga Germans, 1860–1917* (Lincoln NE, 1988).

Löwe, H.-D. *The Tsars and the Jews. Reform, Reaction and Anti-Semitism in Imperial Russia 1772–1917* (Chur, 1993).

Marks, S. G. *Road to Power. The Trans-Siberian Railroad and the Colonization of Asian Russia 1850–1917* (London, 1991).

McDonald, D. M. *United Government and Foreign Policy in Russia, 1900–1914* (Cambridge MA, 1992).

Menning, B. W. *Bayonets before Bullets. The Imperial Russian Army, 1861–1914* (Bloomington, 1992).

Miller, F. A. *Dmitrii Miliutin and the Reform Era in Russia* (Nashville, 1968).

Morgan, G. *Anglo-Russian Rivalry in Central Asia 1810–1895* (London, 1981).

Nish, I. *The Origins of the Russo-Japanese War* (Harlow, 1985).

Petrovich, M. B. *The Emergence of Russian Panslavism 1856–1870* (New York, 1956).

Pierce, R. A. *Russian Central Asia, 1867–1917. A Study in Colonial Rule* (Berkeley, 1960).

Polvinen, T. *Imperial Borderland. Bobrikov and the Attempted Russification of Finland 1898–1904* (London, 1995).

Ragsdale, H. (ed.) *Imperial Russian Foreign Policy* (Cambridge, 1993).

Rogger, H. *Jewish Policies and Right-Wing Politics in Imperial Russia* (London, 1986).

Rywkin, M. (ed.) *Russian Colonial Expansion to 1917* (London, 1988).

Stephan, J. J. *The Russian Far East. A History* (Stanford, 1994).

Subtelny, O. *Ukraine. A History* (Toronto, 1988).

Taylor, A. J. P. *The Struggle for Mastery in Europe 1848–1918* (Oxford, 1954).

Thaden, E. C. *Russia's Western Borderlands, 1710–1870* (Princeton, 1984).

Thaden, E. C. (ed.) *Russification in the Baltic Provinces and Finland,*

1855–1914 (Princeton, 1981).

Wildman, A. K. *The End of the Russian Imperial Army* 2 vols (Princeton, 1980 and 1987).

Wood, A. (ed.) *The History of Siberia. From Russian Conquest to Revolution* (London, 1991).

Revolution

Acton, E. *Rethinking the Russian Revolution* (London, 1990).

Browder, R. P. and Kerensky, A. (eds) *The Russian Provisional Government, 1917. Documents* (Stanford, 1961).

Ferro, M. *The Russian Revolution of 1917: The Fall of Tsarism and the Origins of Bolshevik Power* (Englewood Cliffs, 1972).

—— *The Bolshevik Revolution. A Social History of the Russian Revolution* (London, 1980).

Gill, G. J. *Peasants and Government in the Russian Revolution* (London, 1979).

Hasegawa, T. *The February Revolution* (Seattle, 1981).

Keep, J. L. H. *The Russian Revolution. A Study in Mass Mobilization* (London, 1976).

Mandel, D. *The Petrograd Workers and the Fall of the Old Regime* (London, 1983).

Read, C. *From Tsar to Soviets. The Russian People and their Revolution, 1917–21* (London, 1996).

Service, R. (ed.) *Society and Politics in the Russian Revolution* (London, 1992).

White, J. D. *The Russian Revolution 1917–1921. A Short History* (London, 1994).

INDEX

Afghanistan, 104, 107, 135
agrarian reform, 35, 36, 41, 53, 68, 163
agriculture, 39-79 *passim*, 86, 145, 147, 163
Akhmatova, A. A.(1889–1966), 100
Aksakov, I. S. (1823–86), 123
Alexander II (1818–81), 2–3, 15–17, 19, 20, 41, 47–9, 115, 116, 124, 126, 162
Alexander III (1845–94), 2, 5, 9, 11, 17, 19, 22, 26, 74, 115, 118, 119, 123, 132
Alexandra, Empress (1872–1918), 152
Amur, river, 105
Anglo-Russian agreement (1907), 135
army, 14, 32, 33, 43, 61, 67, 97, 106, 109, 119, 124–5, 134, 139–47, 154, 158–9, 164
Association of Trade and Industry, 144
Austria-Hungary, 39, 46, 67, 123, 126–32, 135–8, 140–2, 164

backwardness, 24
Baku, 29, 90
Balkans, 121, 122, 127–31, 135–8
Baltic Germans, 112, 118
Baltic provinces, 14, 48, 75, 95, 111–12, 115, 117, 118, 119–20
Beseda, 27
Bismarck, Otto von (1815–98), 127, 128, 130, 131

Black Sea, 122, 127, 128, 130, 138, 141, 142
Blok, A. A. (1880–1921), 100
Bloody Sunday (1905), 30, 157
Bobrikov, N. I. (1839–1904), 116, 120
Bokhara, 104
Bolshevik party, 25, 85, 161
books, 17, 93, 98, 119
Bosnia, 129–30, 135
Britain, 39, 105, 107–8, 126, 128, 130, 131, 133, 135, 138, 143, 164
budget, 64–6, 124, 125
Bulgaria, 129, 131, 136
Bulygin, A. D. (1851–1919), 26
bureaucrats, 5, 18

Caucasus, 106, 110
censorship, 14–15, 20, 30, 148
Central Asia, 80, 103, 104, 107–9, 119, 128, 135, 138
Chekhov, A. P. (1860–1904), 76, 99
Cheliabinsk, 104
Chernigov, 18
Chernyshevskii, N. G. (1828–89), 21, 98
Chicherin, B. N. (1828–1904), 56
China, 105–8, 133
civil servants, 88, 112
clergy, 40, 75, 79–80, 90
Committee of Ministers, 2
Congress of Berlin (1878), 39, 121, 130, 136
Constantinople, 122, 129, 137

Index